Seco... ...

PRACTICAL HOMICIDE INVESTIGATION

Checklist and Field Guide

Vernon J. Geberth

CRC Press
Taylor & Francis Group
Boca Raton London New York

CRC Press is an imprint of the
Taylor & Francis Group, an **informa** business

CRC Press
Taylor & Francis Group
6000 Broken Sound Parkway NW, Suite 300
Boca Raton, FL 33487-2742

© 2014 by Taylor & Francis Group, LLC
CRC Press is an imprint of Taylor & Francis Group, an Informa business

No claim to original U.S. Government works

Printed on acid-free paper
Version Date: 20130626

Printed and bound in India by Replika Press Pvt. Ltd.

International Standard Book Number-13: 978-1-4665-9188-2 (Paperback)

This book contains information obtained from authentic and highly regarded sources. Reasonable efforts have been made to publish reliable data and information, but the author and publisher cannot assume responsibility for the validity of all materials or the consequences of their use. The authors and publishers have attempted to trace the copyright holders of all material reproduced in this publication and apologize to copyright holders if permission to publish in this form has not been obtained. If any copyright material has not been acknowledged please write and let us know so we may rectify in any future reprint.

Except as permitted under U.S. Copyright Law, no part of this book may be reprinted, reproduced, transmitted, or utilized in any form by any electronic, mechanical, or other means, now known or hereafter invented, including photocopying, microfilming, and recording, or in any information storage or retrieval system, without written permission from the publishers.

For permission to photocopy or use material electronically from this work, please access www.copyright.com (http://www.copyright.com/) or contact the Copyright Clearance Center, Inc. (CCC), 222 Rosewood Drive, Danvers, MA 01923, 978-750-8400. CCC is a not-for-profit organization that provides licenses and registration for a variety of users. For organizations that have been granted a photocopy license by the CCC, a separate system of payment has been arranged.

Trademark Notice: Product or corporate names may be trademarks or registered trademarks, and are used only for identification and explanation without intent to infringe.

Visit the Taylor & Francis Web site at
http://www.taylorandfrancis.com

and the CRC Press Web site at
http://www.crcpress.com

Table of Contents

The Checklist Approach to Homicide Investigation

I created this *Checklist and Field Guide* based on the textbook *Practical Homicide Investigation: Tactics, Procedures, and Forensic Techniques*, which is recognized as the "bible of homicide investigation." It is the most comprehensive textbook available and contains many case examples as well as forensic procedures, wound recognition techniques, protocols, and numerous references and checklists.

This **newly revised** *Checklist and Field Guide* contains the most current information and updates on technology considerations in ascertaining information from various electronic devices as well as state-of-the-art anatomical graphics in full color to assist the investigator in describing any injuries or wounds to the body. I want to give a special "Thank you" to a professional friend, Brian Wilson, director of production at Medical Legal Art (www.doereport.com), who provided the excellent graphic and illustrative images throughout this *Field Guide*.

The *Checklist and Field Guide* provides first responders, police officers, investigators, medical examiners, coroners, CSIs, and police supervisors with practical checklists which focus on tactics, procedures, and forensic techniques in sudden and violent death inquiries to assure that a proper and complete investigation is undertaken.

These checklists have been placed within this durable and easy-to-use reference notebook. The table of contents indexes the checklists by duty assignment or subject, with the corresponding page number in large print for quick reference in the field.

There are checklists for various types of deaths which indicate exactly what the responder has to do and how to do it. The *Checklist and Field Guide* provides protocols for suicide and equivocal death investigation, final exit suicide and suicide-by-cop cases, arson and fire investigation, autoerotic (sexual asphyxia) investigation, sudden infant death syndrome (SIDS) investigation, Munchausen syndrome by proxy investigation, police action shooting investigations (officer-involved shootings, or OISs), and a homicide supervisor's checklist.

At the Crime Scene

Any item *can* and *may* constitute physical evidence; therefore, it is imperative that nothing be touched or moved at the scene before the arrival of the investigators.

- ☐ If something at the scene needs to be immediately secured or removed before it is destroyed or lost, the officer handling the evidence must document its original location, appearance, condition, and any other feature that might affect the investigation.
- ☐ The officer must be sure to inform the homicide detective of the item's original position so that it does not lose its evidentiary value.

Remember: Once an item of evidence has been moved or altered, it is impossible to restore it to its original position or condition.

Secure and Protect the Crime Scene and Area

The cardinal rule in homicide cases is to *protect and preserve the crime scene*. However, before a crime scene can be protected, it must be identified as such. For the officer to make an intelligent evaluation of the crime scene, he or she must have an idea of what constitutes physical evidence and where the boundaries of the scene should be established in order to protect the evidence. The first police representative at the crime scene is usually the patrol officer. His or her first responsibility is to determine whether the victim is alive. Upon confirming that the victim is dead, an assessment is then made to determine boundaries.

Always secure the most property you can physically control.

Determining the Dimensions of the Homicide Crime Scene

The homicide supervisor and/or the investigator should stop and observe the area as a whole, noting everything possible before entering the actual crime scene for a detailed examination.

Practically speaking, at this stage of the investigation, it is next to impossible to know the exact boundaries of the scene. The best course of action for the officer to follow is

- [ ] Clear the largest area possible. The scene can always be narrowed later.
- [ ] Make a quick and objective evaluation of the scene based on
  a. Location of the body
  b. Presence of any physical evidence
  c. Eyewitness statements
  d. Presence of natural boundaries (a room, house, hallway, enclosed park)
- [ ] Keep in mind the possibility of multiple series of crime scenes.
- [ ] If the crime scene is indoors, the job of making this determination and securing the scene is relatively easy to accomplish.
- [ ] If the scene is outdoors, the determination will have to be based on the type of location, pedestrian and vehicular traffic, crowds, paths of entry and exit, weather conditions, and many other factors peculiar to that specific location.

Remember: Do it right the first time. You only get one chance.

The Patrol Officer's Duties

First Officer's Duties upon Arrival

- [ ] Determine whether the victim is dead or alive and take necessary action.
- [ ] Apprehend the perpetrator, if still present, and make appropriate notifications if he or she is escaping or has escaped.
- [ ] Safeguard the crime scene and detain any witnesses or suspects.

Remember: The individual who first reported the incident may later become a suspect, and the exact words he or she used may become critical to the case.

Protection of Life

The first officer should examine the victim for life signs:

☐ Breath stoppage
☐ Cessation of pulse (See Figure 1.)
☐ Eye reflexes

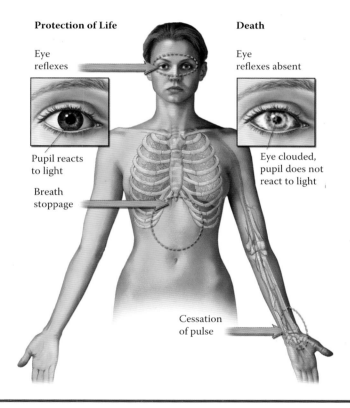

FIGURE 1   A pulse can be detected by placing the tips of one's fingers on the undersurface of the radial bone. In addition, the pulse can also be detected by placing one's fingertips on the temple or flat portion of the side of the victim's forehead. Illustration courtesy of Brian Wilson, Medical Legal Art, © 2005, www.doereport.com. Permission from Vernon Geberth, *Practical Homicide Investigation: Tactics, Procedures, and Forensic Techniques*, 4th ed. (Boca Raton, FL: CRC Press, 2006), 37–38.

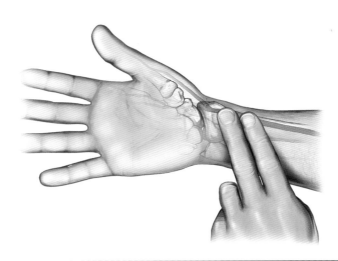

FIGURE 1 (continued) A pulse can be detected by placing the tips of one's fingers on the under-surface of the radial bone. In addition, the pulse can also be detected by placing one's fingertips on the temple or flat portion of the side of the victim's forehead. Illustration courtesy of Brian Wilson, Medical Legal Art, © 2005, www.doereport.com. Permission from Vernon Geberth, *Practical Homicide Investigation: Tactics, Procedures, and Forensic Techniques*, 4th ed. (Boca Raton, FL: CRC Press, 2006), 37–38.

Patrol Officer Establishing the Crime Scene

☐ Clear the largest area possible. The scene can always be narrowed later.
☐ Make a quick and objective evaluation of the scene based on
   a. Location of the body
   b. Presence of any physical evidence
   c. Eyewitness statements
   d. Presence of natural boundaries (a room, house, hallway, enclosed park, etc.)
☐ Wear latex gloves and shoe covers, if practical.
☐ Keep in mind the possibility of a *multiple series* of crime scenes.

Protecting the Crime Scene

The homicide crime scene must be protected from entry by unnecessary or unauthorized persons so that physical evidence will not be altered, moved, destroyed, lost, or contaminated. All other police officers, including supervisory personnel, who do not have a specific or valid reason for being at the crime scene should be regarded as *unauthorized persons*.

The scene should be secured by the use of *ropes, barricades, autos, additional officers*, and even *volunteers from the crowd* if necessary. The use of *crime scene cards* and reflective ribbon can be effective scene indicators.

I suggest that the officers establish *two* crime scenes.

☐ The *first or primary crime scene* is the location where the actual event occurred, or the area where you expect to recover physical evidence. *This primary scene must be protected from further contamination by first responders.* The inner area is *ONLY* for crime scene personnel and investigators.

☐ The *second or secure-area crime scene* is an area set aside from the general public. This area is established for the officials who will be required to conduct the investigation. *This can be called a* security zone *or* staging area. See Figure 2 for examples of two crime scene areas.

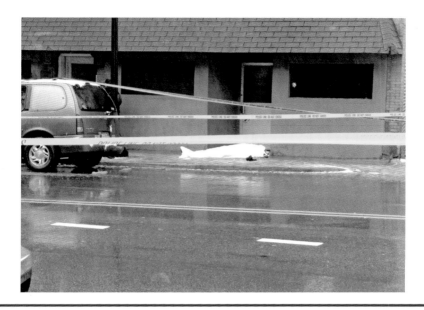

FIGURE 2   Example of the two crime scene area principle. The interior of the crime scene is cordoned off with red tape. The exterior of the crime scene is cordoned off with yellow tape. Courtesy of Detective Mark Czworniak, Chicago Police Department.

The Crime Scene Sign-In Sheet

Figure 3 is an example of a crime sign-in sheet for homicides.

Practical Homicide Investigation®

Crime Scene Sign-In Sheet

(To be posted at the entrance of the perimeter of the Crime)

NAME	DATE & TIME	AGENCY/DEPARTMENT

Officer-In-Charge

FIGURE 3 A crime sign-in sheet for a criminal investigation.

The First Officer Initiates the Homicide Investigation
Recommended Procedures to Initiate the Investigation

The first officer who confronts by the homicide crime scene has a very involved responsibility. Although the formal investigation will be conducted by detectives or the criminal investigator, it is the first *officer* who has the responsibility of initiating the investigation. I have provided four practical rules of procedure which may be used as a guide in initiating a professional homicide investigation.

- ☐ Arrest the perpetrator if you can determine by direct inquiry or observation that he or she is the suspect. (As a general rule, do not question him or her at this stage.)
- ☐ Detain all persons present at the scene.
- ☐ Attempt to assess and determine the entire area of the *crime scene*, including paths of entry and exit and any areas that may include evidence.
- ☐ Isolate the area and *protect the scene*. Seek assistance if necessary. Notifications must be made to superiors, investigators, and specialized units. (Use crime scene cards or tape to.)

Patrol Officer's Quicklist

A Arrest the perpetrator if possible.
D Detain and identify witnesses and/or suspects.
A Assess the crime scene.
P Protect the crime scene.
T Take notes.

The Patrol Officer's Checklist

As a practical matter, the first officer's responsibilities in the preliminary investigation of homicide are divided into three specific duties:

1. Preserve life.
2. Arrest the suspect.
3. Protect the scene.

I have provided the following checklist of first-officer duties in order to assist the officer at the scene by refreshing his or her memory as to what vital information should be secured.

Initial Call and Receipt of Information

- ☐ Record exact time and type of call patrol unit received. (In systems using modern computerized and recorded radio transmissions, the unit can check with Communications.)
- ☐ If first notification is received in person, detain this person for investigators. If unable to detain for some reason, obtain sufficient identification and information for the follow-up investigator.
- ☐ If practical, review the actual 911 call for service, and make notes as to caller's demeanor.

Arrival at the Homicide Crime Scene

- ☐ Record the exact time of your arrival and/or notify Communications that you are on the scene.
- ☐ Enter the immediate crime scene area to view the victim. (Only one officer should enter the scene unless the call is an emergency call and the offender may still be at the scene.) Use only one path of entry and exit. *Look up, down, and all around.*
- ☐ Be careful not to trample evidence on the ground, and be cognizant of evidence above you.
- ☐ Determine if victim is alive or dead.
- ☐ Arrest the perpetrator if present.
- ☐ If there is a possibility of life, summon ambulance and apply appropriate first-aid procedures.
- ☐ If circumstances indicate the victim is near death or dying, attempt to obtain a dying declaration.
- ☐ If ambulance crew is present before your arrival, determine if the crew or anyone else moved the body or any items within the crime scene. If any items were moved, record the following:
  - ☐ What alterations were made
  - ☐ When the alterations were made

□ Purpose of the movement
□ Person(s) who made the alterations
□ Record the names, serial numbers, and hospital of all ambulance crew present at the scene.
□ If the victim is dead, record the official time of pronouncement by ambulance attendant.
□ If suspect has just fled the scene, initiate a wanted alarm.
□ Record any alterations to the crime scene that were made as a matter of investigative necessity. For example:
  □ Lights turned on or off
  □ Doors opened, closed, locked, or unlocked
  □ Body moved or cut down
  □ Windows opened, closed, locked, or unlocked
  □ Furniture moved
  □ Anything touched
  □ Gas turned off, appliances turned off, motor of vehicle on or off

Protection of the Crime Scene

□ Attempt to assess the entire crime scene, including paths of entry and exit, and any areas that may include evidence. (Remember the possibility of a multiple crime scene.)
□ Establish a perimeter; secure and protect the scene by isolation and physical barriers such as ropes, cones, and other equipment as necessary.
□ Record names, addresses, dates of birth, telephone numbers, etc., of all persons present at the crime scene.
□ Remove all persons from the immediate area. (Be careful not to chase off witnesses or the perpetrator, who may still be present.)
□ If victim is removed from scene by ambulance, an officer should accompany victim to the hospital, riding in the rear with the victim (for possible dying declaration).
□ An officer should remain at the scene in order to provide for its security.
□ If the victim's clothes are removed at the hospital, an officer should maintain control of them (the victim's clothes are evidence).

☐ Request additional units as needed to protect the scene.
☐ If it is necessary that a clergy member or doctor enter the scene, have an officer accompany this person through the designated path of entry, and caution him or her about contamination and/or alteration.

Notifications

☐ Make notifications by telephone if possible (police radios are often monitored by the press).
☐ Never, unless absolutely necessary, use a telephone inside the crime scene. Such necessity would involve a life-or-death situation, the need for immediate transmission of alarms, etc.
☐ Notify the investigators or homicide division.
☐ Record time of notification and who was notified.
☐ Establish a temporary headquarters outside the central crime scene, preferably a location with two phones, one for incoming calls, one for outgoing. In addition, you can use cell phones for communications between and among investigators and headquarters.
☐ Broadcast any alarms for suspects or descriptions of perpetrators from the command post to guarantee uniformity and possibility of verification.
☐ Notify Communications of the telephone numbers of the command post as well as the cell phone numbers of members at the scene to facilitate communications between the various units.

Preliminary Investigation

☐ Initiate and maintain a chronological log recording the names, shield numbers, and commands of any police officers entering the crime scene. In addition, record the names, addresses, etc., of any civilians who may have to enter, as well as names, titles, and serial numbers of any ambulance personnel. This log should reflect the entry and exit of any person who enters the crime scene.
☐ Isolate and separate witnesses or suspects. Do not permit any conversations relative to the crime. Hold witnesses and suspects for the investigators.

- [ ] Establish a single path of entry and exit based on observation of the scene.
- [ ] For any civilians at the scene, record identifying information and their knowledge of the crime.
- [ ] Do not touch, move, or alter anything in the scene. If you do, record it.
- [ ] Do not smoke in the crime scene.
- [ ] Do not flush toilets or run tap water in sinks or bathtubs. If it has been done, record it.
- [ ] Refer all newspaper and media inquiries to the investigators.
- [ ] Stand by for investigators, and assist them as required.
- [ ] Advise and inform investigators of all that has transpired since the arrival of the first officer.

The Suspect in Custody

If the first arriving officers take a person into custody and the person wants to talk, remember to advise that person of his or her Miranda rights.

Miranda Warning

1. You have the right to remain silent.
2. Anything you say can and will be used against you in a court of law.
3. You have the right to talk to a lawyer and have him present with you while you are being questioned.
4. If you cannot afford to hire a lawyer, one will be appointed to represent you before any questioning, if you wish one.

Waiver

After the warning and in order to secure a waiver, the following questions should be asked and an affirmative reply secured to each question.

1. Do you understand each of these rights I have explained to you?
2. Having these rights in mind, do you wish to talk to us now?

Determine if the suspect is armed (search for weapons). If a weapon is recovered, record description and location. Maintain custody pending arrival of investigators, who will instruct as to vouchering and disposition.

☐ Handcuff suspect and isolate him/her from any witnesses and/or associates. (Use rear handcuff method.)

☐ If suspect is arrested outside the crime scene, do not return him/her to the scene.

☐ If suspect is arrested inside the crime scene, remove him/her immediately. (Remember scene contamination.)

☐ Note and preserve any evidence found on suspect, advise investigators.

☐ Do not permit suspect to wash hands or use toilet (you may lose evidence).

☐ Do not permit any conversation between the suspect and any other parties.

☐ Do not initiate any interrogation (wait for the investigators). However, in certain types of homicides the first officer will take statements. Make sure, however, that suspect has been warned of his or her rights before taking any statement. As a general rule, however, conduct no interrogations.

☐ Carefully record all spontaneous statements (under the *Res gestae* rule).

☐ Observe and record behavior of suspect (e.g., nervous, erratic, emotional, unemotional, drunk, under the influence of drugs, any unusual behavior).

Suicide and Accidental Deaths

☐ If death appears to be suicidal or accidental, handle as homicide, pending arrival of investigators. All death investigations should be treated as homicide investigations.

    ☐ Secure immediate scene, detain witnesses.

    ☐ Preserve all evidence (e.g., notes, weapons, pills, vials, drugs) in their original position.

    ☐ Notify investigators.

    ☐ If vehicles are involved, do not allow their removal until photos have been taken by crime scene technicians or crime scene investigation (CSI) personnel.

    ☐ If suicide is by hanging and death is evident, do not cut body down.

    ☐ If body is cut down because death is not evident, make cut above the knot.

☐ If relatives are present, get any background information, which may assist investigators.

Remember: At this stage of the investigation, the only evidence that should be collected by the patrol officer is eyewitness or testimonial in nature, such as *res gestae*, which refers to spontaneous utterances of a suspect.

The Preliminary Investigation at the Scene

The Detectives

The information within this section of the *Checklist and Field Guide* is intended to help the detective and detective supervisor at the homicide crime scene to systematically check and review all the facts applicable to the investigation.

Initial Receipt of Information

☐ Date and time of notification
☐ Method of transmission (e.g. telephone, radio, or in person)
☐ Name, rank, shield number, and other data identifying the person who is reporting the information to detectives
☐ Description of the death scene event (homicide, suicide, accident, or natural)
☐ People present at the scene (law enforcement, medical, family, etc.)
☐ Complete details of the information and event

Prior to Leaving for the Crime Scene, Instruct Patrol To

☐ Preserve the crime scene.
☐ Hold all witnesses and/or suspects.
☐ Avoid using telephones in the crime scene.
☐ Initiate a personnel log accounting for all activities at the scene, including identification of all persons who have had access to the scene.
☐ Record the license numbers and vehicle information of all autos in the area of the crime scene (if applicable).

Arrival at the Scene

Investigators are rarely the first officers at the scene of a homicide. The body is usually discovered by friends, relatives, or citizens, who in turn notify the police or call for an ambulance. The presence of first responders, including police and fire personnel as well as emergency medical services (EMS), can create chaos and confusion at the crime scene. The response of the homicide investigator and detective supervisor must be methodical.

Upon arriving at the scene, the investigator should note the following:

- ☐ Time of arrival
- ☐ The exact address of the scene
- ☐ Persons present (officers, ambulance or medical people, relatives, friends, etc.)
- ☐ The condition and position of the body (personally verify death)

The investigator should also:

- ☐ Obtain preliminary information concerning the death.
- ☐ Determine who entered the scene and what, if anything, was touched or disturbed.
- ☐ Document EMS activities, and identify all EMS personnel.
- ☐ Ascertain what changes were made to the body and the scene by EMS, and document,
- ☐ Also, collect any items of evidence that may have been disturbed during life-saving efforts.

Legal Authority

- ☐ Determine your legal authority to be present in and to conduct the death scene examination.
- ☐ Initially when responding to an emergency, there is no search warrant requirement. However, at some point, the "emergency exigency" for your presence at the scene will expire.

- [ ] What is your continued authority to remain in the scene and collect evidence?
- [ ] Obtain a search warrant, permissive authorization, or consent to search, or determine that there is no reasonable expectation of privacy.

Follow the Investigation Checklist

See the "The Investigative Checklist" section.

- [ ] Refrain from entering the scene and/or disturbing, touching, or using any item found therein. *Never use the crime scene as a command post or the telephone as a communications center.* Figure 4 shows examples of crime scene tape in use.
- [ ] In communicating with the station house or headquarters, the first officer should *not*, unless absolutely necessary, use a telephone instrument at the scene. This necessity *should* be determined by common sense and priorities. Most officers have cellular service through the department or carry their own cell phones.
- [ ] The first officers should instead establish a temporary command post, preferably outside the central crime scene. There should be at least two phones available, one for incoming calls and one for outgoing ones. In the early stages of the investigation, there is a definite need for rapid communication between the various centers of investigation.
- [ ] Identify (and, if possible, retain for questioning) the person who first notified the police.
- [ ] Separate the witnesses to obtain independent statements.
- [ ] Exclude all unauthorized persons from entering the main scene until the arrival of the investigators. This, of course, includes police officers not directly involved in the crime scene investigation. The detective supervisor and the investigator assigned are, of course, allowed entry into the scene for evaluation purposes.
- [ ] Other unavoidable exceptions may include the medical examiner, a doctor, or clergy members. *In any event, establish a pathway in and out to avoid unnecessary disturbance.*

FIGURE 4　Crime scene tape (top) in original packaging and (bottom) in use at a crime scene.

☐ Keep a *chronological log* containing the name, shield number, command, and title of any police official who enters the crime scene; the name, serial number, and hospital of any medical personnel, ambulance drivers, or technicians; and the names and addresses of any civilians who may have entered the crime scene before the arrival of the authorities.

☐ Take notes.

Remember: Never use the crime scene as a command post or the telephone as a communications center.

The Investigative Checklist

The homicide detective faces a monumental task at the crime scene. There are a multitude of duties to perform, and each event needs to be documented according to a routine procedure. This routine procedure is necessary so that valuable information or observations are not overlooked. Although each homicide is distinctive and unique, there are certain basic steps to be pursued at all crime scenes. This *Checklist and Field Guide* is designed to be utilized by detectives involved in the investigation of sudden and violent death. Although extensive, it is not all-inclusive. The investigator is advised to simply utilize this *Checklist* as a guide to refresh memory.

> **Remember: The fundamental rule in homicide investigation is the documentation of events in the investigator's notebook.**

Documentation of the Initial Report

Initial Receipt of Information

- ☐ Date and time of initial report
- ☐ Method of transmission—report received by whom?
- ☐ Reporting party—officer, dispatcher, etc.
- ☐ Complete details

Arrival at the Homicide Scene

- ☐ Record exact time of arrival.
- ☐ Record the exact address of the crime scene.
- ☐ Record outside weather and temperature conditions.
- ☐ Record outside lighting conditions.
- ☐ Interview the first officer and other police personnel at the scene to determine the sequence of events since their arrival.
- ☐ Crime discovered by whom? Date and time of initial call? Complete details of initial police report.
- ☐ Determine the scope of the patrol officer's initial investigation at the scene.

☐ Protection of the crime scene
☐ Notifications, alarms, teletypes, "Be on the Lookout" (BOLOs)
☐ Preliminary investigative results
☐ Record persons present at the scene:
    ☐ Police officers and law enforcement personnel
    ☐ Ambulance and/or emergency personnel
    ☐ Family and/or friends of victim
    ☐ Witnesses—including persons detained by patrol officers
        ☐ Keep witnesses separated.
        ☐ Provide for witness security and availability.

Preliminary Inspection of the Body at the Crime Scene

☐ Victim pedigree—name and address if known (include the following: sex, race, and age)
☐ Location of the victim: description of body and scene
☐ Have the patrol officer personally escort you through the scene to the body using the same path used by responding police.
☐ Personally determine and verify death.
☐ Note condition of the body.
☐ Ascertain whether or not any suspects are in custody. (See the procedure in the "The Suspect in Custody" section.)
☐ Are there any additional victims?
    ☐ Is this a multiple murder? (If *yes*, establish separate case numbers and provide for additional documentation.)
☐ Officially assign an investigator to the case.
☐ If identity of victim(s) is known, get a background check.

Implement Crime Scene Control Procedures

Death scenes are often highly complex and require skilled care and methodical processing. There is no requirement to have a body removed immediately from the scene, and removal can be detrimental if it occurs before a scene is thoroughly examined for evidence.

☐ Determine the scope of the general crime scene—conduct an assessment.
☐ Make a determination of police legal status in crime scene.

- [ ] Take preliminary photographs with a digital camera to "freeze" the crime scene, and provide photos for review by additional investigators as they arrive at the scene.
- [ ] Digital photos are preferred for immediate viewing.
- [ ] Your digital camera's memory card may be subpoenaed at trial.
- [ ] You must account for all consecutive photos on the memory card.
- [ ] Never delete any image from the storage media.
- [ ] Insure that the date and time stamp is correct.
- [ ] Conduct the initial walk-through:
  - [ ] Use protective clothing, including footwear cover, gloves, etc.
  - [ ] Establish paths of entry and exit separate from the offender(s).
  - [ ] Document and safeguard perishable evidence.
- [ ] Determine investigative needs based on a preliminary walk-through; also determine whether additional or specialized personnel will be required. Formulate your process plan based on your observations.
- [ ] Stabilize the scene by identifying and establishing perimeters.
  - [ ] If a crime scene was not established by patrol, secure and protect the scene by isolation:
    - [ ] Use crime scene tape, ropes, barriers, etc.
    - [ ] Establish outside and inside perimeters—only authorized personnel allowed within respective perimeters.
- [ ] Remember the two-crime-scenes theory: The general area is for police and other official personnel at the scene, and the forensic area is where the body as well as any other evidence may be located.
- [ ] Assign patrol officers as needed to effectively safeguard scene.
- [ ] Update and expand crime scene protection as necessary.
- [ ] Is this a multiple scene? Are there additional areas to protect?
- [ ] Establish a single path of entry and exit to the crime scene.
- [ ] Implement procedures to safeguard all evidence found at the scene.

Initiate a Crime Scene Log

- [ ] Assign an officer to obtain the names of all police and emergency personnel who responded to the original call.
- [ ] Assign an officer to record the names of all personnel and civilians involved in the investigation at the crime scene.

☐ Allow no entry to the crime scene except to authorized personnel involved in the official investigation.

☐ Record arrival and departure times of all officials. This includes the medical examiner or coroner, state's attorney, crime scene technicians, etc.

☐ This crime scene log should be delivered to detectives upon release of the crime scene.

Establish a Policy for Crime Scene Integrity

☐ Make a determination relative to obtaining a search warrant prior to any processing of the crime scene.

☐ Coordinate activities at the scene, and direct investigators by fixing responsibility for the performance of certain duties.

☐ Do not touch, move, or alter anything at the scene until full documentation has been completed (observe, describe, record).

☐ Record any alterations to the crime scene that were made as a matter of investigative necessity or emergency police response.

    ☐ Lights turned on or off?

    ☐ Doors opened, closed? Locked or unlocked?

    ☐ Body moved, or body cut down?

    ☐ Windows opened, closed? Locked, or unlocked?

    ☐ Names of all parties who moved the body prior to and during the police presence at the scene.

    ☐ Any furniture moved, or anything touched?

    ☐ Gas turned on or off? Appliances turned on or off?

    ☐ If vehicle involved, is engine off or on? Is the motor cold, cool, warm, or hot?

☐ Do not use any telephone(s) located inside the crime scene.

    ☐ Does the telephone have an answering machine or message capability? Check messages. Check the last number, redial, and listen to messages. Make recording and seal original tape.

    ☐ Does the deceased have a beeper? Check messages. Check the last number, redial, and listen to messages. Make recording, and seal any original recordings.

- ☐ Does the deceased have voice mail? Check messages. Check the last number, redial, and listen to any messages or check the answering service.
- ☐ Check any cell phones and smartphones. Take recordings, seal original tapes, and document.
- ☐ Examine the cell phone only if you are familiar with the operation of that phone. Otherwise, leave the examination of that phone to someone familiar with its operation and function.
- ☐ Recover the phone charger if available.
- ☐ Is there a computer at the crime scene? Check its system, last date of use, documents, disks, hard drive. Consider forensic computer analysis.
  - ☐ Remember that external computer hard drives and storage devices come in all shapes and sizes.
  - ☐ Recover any DVD- or CD-burning equipment as it may be needed to review any recovered DVDs or CDs at the scene.
  - ☐ Check the computer for an answering machine–message modem—check messages, e-mail, and so on.
- ☐ Is there a camera at the crime scene? Process and check film and/or diskettes and/or memory cards. Search for photographs—deceased, friends, activities, etc.
- ☐ Is there a DVD player or VCR? Check all disks, tapes including any in the machine. Note rentals, personal tapes/recordings, etc.—and secure for review.
- ☐ Implement procedures to protect the evidence from damage by weather or exposure or by the presence of police personnel.
- ☐ Do not allow smoking by anyone in the crime scene.
- ☐ Do not turn water on or off, do not flush toilets, do not use any facility in the scene.
- ☐ Record condition of lights, lamps, and electric appliances such as televisions, radios, or clocks that may show programs watched or recorded.

Establish a Command Post or Temporary Headquarters

☐ Select a location out of the central crime scene, preferably a location with two phones: a phone for outgoing calls and a phone for incoming ones. Utilize cell phones for general communications. Use the land lines for security.

☐ Utilize your agency's mobile command van, or request one through mutual aid agreements.

☐ Notify Communications and/or the station house of the telephone numbers of the command post as well as personnel at the scene to facilitate communications between the various units concerned.

☐ Make notifications as necessary from this location:
    ☐ Crime scene technicians
    ☐ Medical examiner, coroner, or representatives
    ☐ Additional investigators or police personnel
    ☐ Prosecutor, district attorney, or solicitor's office

EMS and Ambulance Personnel

☐ If ambulance or EMS personnel were present in the scene before the investigator's arrival, determine if the crew or anyone else moved the body or any other items within the crime scene. If yes, record the following:
    ☐ When the alterations were made
    ☐ Purpose of the movement
    ☐ Person(s) who made the alterations
    ☐ The time of death as pronounced by the ambulance or paramedic crew
    ☐ Consider taking fingerprints of the crew if items in the crime scene were touched or handled by them.
    ☐ Interview the EMS or ambulance crew for details of any action taken as well as their observations.
    ☐ Firefighters and paramedics work odd shifts and schedules. Determine the best time to recontact them.

Initiate a Canvass

- ☐ Initiate a canvass of the immediate area by assigning sufficient personnel to locate any witnesses or persons who may have information about the homicide or death.
- ☐ Assign a supervisor or coordinator to organize the canvass.
    - ☐ Utilize canvass control sheets.
- ☐ Assure that canvassers are provided with all information from the investigation and scene so that they may properly solicit information from prospective witnesses. (This includes photos of the deceased taken in life, if available.)
- ☐ Have investigators check vehicles and record registration numbers of autos in the immediate area.
- ☐ Require official reports from canvassers indicating:
    - ☐ Negative locations (i.e., locations with no results)
    - ☐ Locations that have been canvassed, indicating the number of persons residing therein to include possible visitors as well as residents.
    - ☐ Positive locations for possible follow-up and re-interview
    - ☐ Information relating to the event being canvassed
    - ☐ Utilize the canvass questionnaire forms.

Note: **Attempt to conduct further canvasses on the same day of the week as the incident, at approximately the same time as when the incident occurred, in order to cover the behavioral patterns of persons to be canvassed.**

Canvass Questionnaire Form

Canvass Questionnaire
(Identify Yourself and Purpose of Canvass)

Name: (last)   (first)   (middle)   Date of Birth:

Address: Phone:

Employment (company name—type of work):   Address: Phone:

Other Residents of This Address: (names and ages)

Did you know of the offense?   ☐ Yes   ☐ No

How did you first learn of it? (when?)

Did you know the victim?   ☐ Yes   ☐ No

What was your relationship with the victim? (if knew, date, time, and location last seen ?? talked to)

Were you on the crime scene at anytime? (explain)

What knowledge do you have of the crime?

Typed statement taken from this witness?   ☐ Yes   ☐ No

Reporting officer   (name)   (unit)   (date)   (time)

continued

Canvass Questionnaire Form

Canvass Questionnaire

Street, Avenue, Road, etc. _____

Number (or name if no number) _____

If Apartment or Office Building (name) _____

Occupants (full name and age)   Questionnaire
                                                           Completed

1. _____   Yes—No

2. _____   Yes—No

3. _____   Yes—No

4. _____   Yes—No

5. _____   Yes—No

6. _____   Yes—No

Officer Recording _____

Time _____ Date _____

Source: Reprinted with permission from Vernon Geberth, *Practical Homicide Investigation: Tactics, Procedures, and Forensic Techniques*, 4th ed. (Boca Raton, FL: CRC Press, 2006), 80–81.

Weapons

If a weapon is discovered, do the following:

- ☐ Firearms—do not attempt to unload.
- ☐ Record where the weapon is located.
- ☐ Safeguard the weapon for forensic examination (this includes not only ballistics but operability as well).
- ☐ Have the weapon photographed before further examination.
- ☐ If weapon was a firearm, consider an examination of the suspect's hands for residue analysis (GSR) testing.

- [ ] Determine the origin of the weapon. (Does it come from the premises? Does it belong to the deceased? Etc.)
- [ ] Determine if any blood or any other trace evidence is on the weapon.

The Suspect in Custody

- [ ] Remember that the suspect is part of the crime scene (theory of "transfer and exchange" and "Locard's Principle").
- [ ] If the suspect is arrested and present at the scene, make sure that he or she is immediately removed from the crime scene and not returned to the scene unless the clothing of the suspect is secured. This procedure is necessary to prevent crime scene contamination.
- [ ] Safeguard all evidence found on the suspect, including blood, weapons, debris, soil, proceeds of the crime, etc.
- [ ] Ensure that the suspect does not wash his or her hands, or engage in any conduct which may alter or destroy evidence.
- [ ] Note any injuries to the suspect, and record them with black-and-white film with a rule of measure included as well as color photographs indicating these injuries or marks with appropriate anatomical reference photographs.
- [ ] Record any spontaneous statements made by the suspect(s).
- [ ] Do not permit any conversation between the suspect(s) and any other parties present.
- [ ] Guard your investigative conversations in the presence of the suspect(s).

The Suspect in Custody: Interrogation at the Scene

If the suspect is in custody at the scene, and circumstances indicate that immediate interrogation of the subject would be beneficial to the investigation, the following steps should be taken:

- [ ] Advise the suspect of his or her rights under the Miranda ruling prior to any custodial interrogation (this should be done from a Miranda rights card or Miranda form; see Table 1).

- ☐ Determine if the suspect fully understands his or her rights.
- ☐ Obtain an intelligent waiver of these rights from the suspect prior to any questioning.
- ☐ Document this procedure in the investigative notebook.
- ☐ Allow the suspect to make a full statement.
- ☐ Record and reduce this statement to writing, and have the suspect sign it.
- ☐ Keep the suspect isolated at all times from witnesses, other suspects, prisoners, and any personnel not connected with the investigation.
- ☐ Advise any officers transporting the suspect not to engage the suspect in any conversation or questioning. However, if during transport the suspect makes any statement, the officers should document this information.
- ☐ If the suspect is brought to the police station, he or she should be placed in a separate holding cell.
- ☐ Alibi statements should be documented and recorded in the investigator's notebook.
- ☐ Any self-serving statements should also be recorded and documented, in the event the suspect later changes his or her story.
- ☐ Before beginning crime scene process, make an assessment regarding search warrant requirements.
- ☐ Except for emergency situations, the crime scene search should not be undertaken until all photographs, sketches, measurements, dusting for prints, and written documentation have been completed.

Crime Scene Photographs

The following photographs should be taken:

- ☐ Photos of the entire location where the homicide took place
- ☐ Photos of contiguous areas and sites
- ☐ Photographs of the crowd or any bystanders—surreptitiously
- ☐ Photos of suspect(s) and/or witnesses, if applicable
  - ☐ Photos of suspect's clothing and shoes
  - ☐ Photos of any of suspect's injuries (to body, face, hands, etc.)

☐ Do not add any chalk marks or markers prior to taking the original crime scene photographs. Markers can be added later for close-up shots.

☐ Take photos from the general to the specific.

Documentation of Crime Scene Photographs

☐ Date and time at which photos are taken; Digital cameras automatically record this information.

☐ Exact location of photographs

☐ Description of item photographed

☐ Compass direction (north, south, east, or west)

☐ Focus distance

☐ Type of film and camera utilized

☐ Lighting and weather conditions

☐ Number of exposures

☐ Identification of photographer

☐ Eliminate extraneous objects, including any police equipment.

☐ Show the relationship of the scene to its surroundings.

 ☐ Outdoor scenes: Include fixed objects as they relate to the scene from eye level.

 ☐ Indoor scenes: Include immovable objects in the room such as doors and windows to "fix" the body to the crime scene.

☐ Recommended crime scene photographs:

 ☐ Front entrance of building

 ☐ Entrance to the room or apartment where the deceased is found

 ☐ Two (2) full-body views

 ☐ A general view of the body and crime scene

 ☐ A close-up shot of the body

 ☐ Photos of any visible wounds

 ☐ If the body has been removed, photos of the body's original location.

 ☐ Photos of possible entrance or escape routes used

 ☐ Areas where any force was used for entry or exit

 ☐ Area and close-up views of any physical evidence such as bloodstains, weapons, shell casings, hairs, fibers

□ Fingerprints (plastic, bloodstained, and latent)—as well as any "lifts"—should be photographed before removal.
□ After body has been moved, additional photos should be taken:
　　□ Areas beneath the body
　　□ Any additional evidence found beneath the body

The Crime Scene Sketch

□ Make a simple line drawing of the crime scene, either in the investigative notebook or on a separate sheet of paper.
□ Draw the body, showing its position in the scene by fixing the position through triangulation or another method of measurement.
□ Indicate the position of the victim's:
　　□ Head
　　□ Torso
　　□ Arms (shoulder, elbow, and wrist joints)
　　□ Legs (hips, knees, and ankles)
□ Note distances and relationships to any objects in the immediate vicinity of the body that may have played a role in the death.
□ The following information should be included:
　　□ Measurements and distance
　　□ A title block consisting of
　　　　□ Name and title of sketcher
　　　　□ Date and time the sketch was made
　　　　□ Classification of the crime
　　　　□ Identification of victim(s)
　　　　□ Agency's case number(s)
　　　　□ Names of persons assisting in taking measurements
　　Precise address of the location sketched, with compass north indicated
　　　　□ A legend to identify any objects or articles in the scene
　　　　□ A scale, to depict measurements used

Commercially available crime scene drawing programs are available for PCs, tablets, and/or smartphones (e.g., CoralDRAW.com)

The Crime Scene Search

- ☐ Establish the perimeters of the crime scene and document this location by crime scene photographs and sketches, including written documentation.
- ☐ Reconstruct aspects of the crime in formulating the search.
- ☐ Ascertain the legal basis for the search prior to any seizure of evidence.
- ☐ Secure a warrant if necessary.
- ☐ Visibly locate any physical evidence and determine which evidence should be gathered before any destruction or any alteration takes place.
- ☐ Place flags or markers near vulnerable evidence so it will not be trampled on.
- ☐ Establish the method of search based on your investigative theory, size of the area to be searched, and any other factors that arise while conducting this phase of the inquiry.
- ☐ Areas that should be processed:
    - ☐ The point of entry
    - ☐ The escape route
    - ☐ The suspect and his or her clothing, including injuries
    - ☐ The location of any physical evidence or weapons
    - ☐ A vehicle used in the crime
    - ☐ The suspect's residence
    - ☐ The location where the actual assault leading to death took place
    - ☐ Location from which the body was moved

Dust for Fingerprints

The following areas should be processed for *latent prints*:

- ☐ Areas of entry and exit
- ☐ Weapons or objects which were apparently handled
- ☐ Door handles
- ☐ Telephone instruments
- ☐ Electronics equipment
- ☐ Tablets, iPods, computers, etc.
- ☐ Windows
- ☐ Glasses

- ☐ Light switches
- ☐ Newly damaged areas
- ☐ Objects that may have caused death
- ☐ Objects missing from their original locations

Note that some areas to be processed may require the use of chemical reagents such as fluorscein, hemascein, luminol, ninhydrin, amido black, tetramethylbenzidine, phenolphtalin, or cynoacrylate in order to obtain latent print evidence. Consider these options before dusting.

Description of the Deceased

A complete description of the body should be documented in the investigator's notes, including the following information:

- ☐ The position of the body
- ☐ Sex
- ☐ Race
- ☐ Appearance
- ☐ Age
- ☐ Build
- ☐ Color of hair
- ☐ Description of clothing
- ☐ Presence or absence of any jewelry
- ☐ Evidence of any injuries (bruises, bite marks, wounds, etc.)
- ☐ Condition of the body:
  - ☐ Livor mortis
  - ☐ Rigor mortis
  - ☐ Decomposition (describe in detail)
  - ☐ Blood, wet or dry
  - ☐ Insect activity
  - ☐ Putrefaction
  - ☐ Check body temperature and record ambient temperature.
- ☐ Is the condition of the body consistent with known facts?
- ☐ Note and record the condition of the victim's hands for signs of evidence (defense marks, hairs, fibers, etc.).

- ☐ Note and record any creases and folds on victim's clothing.
- ☐ What is the condition of the victim's pockets?
- ☐ Examine the immediate area surrounding the body for evidence.
- ☐ Record the direction and size of any bloodstains. For more information, see "Bloodstain Pattern Analysis," in Vernon Geberth, *Practical Homicide Investigation: Tactics, Procedures, and Forensic Techniques*, 4th ed. (Boca Raton, FL: CRC Press, 2006), p. 199.
- ☐ Check the clothing and shoes for any trace evidence.

Victim and Hospital Information

- ☐ If victim was removed to a hospital, dispatch investigators, if available, or a patrol unit to obtain the following information:
  - ☐ Name, address, and phone number of the hospital
  - ☐ Attending doctor's: name, address, and phone
  - ☐ Name of officer interviewing the doctor
  - ☐ Doctor's diagnosis
  - ☐ If pronounced dead, time and date. If admitted to the hospital, time and date.
- ☐ Was the victim interviewed—yes or no?
  - ☐ Name of officer conducting interview
  - ☐ Dying declaration?
    - ☐ Obtain witnesses, preferably a doctor or nurse.
- ☐ Obtain names, addresses, phone numbers of all emergency room and hospital personnel involved in treatment.
- ☐ Obtain names, addresses, phone numbers of all ambulance or paramedic personnel involved in emergency and transport.
- ☐ Obtain names, addresses, phone numbers of anyone who accompanied victim to the hospital.
- ☐ Evidence obtained and/or impounded at the hospital:
  - ☐ Establish chain of custody—identity of person at the hospital who impounded any evidence.
  - ☐ Obtain any clothing worn by the deceased for forensic examination.
- ☐ Obtain names of all police personnel at the hospital.

Evidence Process and Control Procedures

- ☐ Ensure that all evidence is properly marked and packaged.
- ☐ Establish a *chain of custody.*
- ☐ Designate a *searching officer* to take charge of all evidence.
- ☐ Record the name and unit designation of all persons participating in the homicide crime scene search.
- ☐ Photograph all evidence in its original position (in situ).
- ☐ Record the position and location of all evidence on the crime scene sketch and in the investigative notebook.
- ☐ Record the name of any officer or person discovering any physical evidence, and the location where it was recovered.
- ☐ Measure the location of any evidence found from two (2) separate fixed points of reference.
- ☐ Weapons:
    - ☐ Are any shell casings present?
    - ☐ Any bullet holes or spent rounds?
    - ☐ Determine how many shots were fired.
    - ☐ Position of bullets in revolver (record by diagram)
    - ☐ Safety on or off?
    - ☐ Is the firearm loaded or unloaded? Any bullet(s) in the chamber?
    - ☐ Weapons may be swabbed for the presence of DNA.
    - ☐ Preserve and package accordingly.
- ☐ Are wounds consistent with the weapon suspected?
- ☐ Is there any trace evidence on the weapon?

Release of the Homicide Crime Scene

Critical decision: Authorities should hold onto the crime scene as long as possible in the event that further processing, investigation, or review becomes necessary as additional information becomes available.

- ☐ Do not release the scene prior to the completion of the canvass and any interviews of witnesses or interrogation of suspect(s).
- ☐ Have the deceased's mailbox searched, and note the date of any mail found therein. Check with the post office for undelivered mail, and record all information.

☐ Note the telephone numbers of any phones at the scene.

☐ If the scene is to be abandoned temporarily during certain investigative procedures, provide for continued crime scene protection during the absence of investigators. The assignment of patrol officers to assist detectives at the crime scene is highly recommended.

☐ Before leaving the crime scene, look over the entire area from the perspective of the defense counsel to make sure you have "covered all the bases."

☐ Seal all practical points of entry, and affix the signature of the sealing officer or investigator. If returning to the scene at a later date, photograph the breaking of the seal and resealing, if required.

☐ Take exit photos. If the scene is sealed by the medical examiner or by crime scene evidence tape, photograph to document that the seals are intact when the scene is released.

☐ Gather all materials used in processing the crime scene, such as film packs, film containers, notes, tape, and evidence containers

  ☐ Cause these materials to be removed from the scene for destruction and disposal at another location.

  ☐ Utilize large plastic garbage bags at the crime scene for disposal of materials generated during the search.

☐ A common practice is to have all personnel who wore latex gloves in the scene write their badge number on the wrist section with a black marker. If a glove is accidentally left on the scene, its origins are readily traceable.

It is important to note that the extent of the crime scene search can be ascertained by the examination of these types of materials if they are left behind at the crime scene by the authorities.

Duties of the Detective Supervisor upon Arrival at the Scene

The detective supervisor or chief investigator, upon arrival, will assume responsibility for conducting the homicide investigation and will replace the initial investigator as the ranking officer in charge of the case.

It is extremely important that the detective supervisor and the homicide investigator not permit themselves to fall into a fixed routine. Previous experience is invaluable but can become a hindrance when allowance is not made for new possibilities.

> **Remember: Each homicide case is distinct and unique and may require a fresh approach or perspective. Keep an open mind.**

Practically speaking, no one at this stage of the investigation has all the answers, nor can anyone know for sure exactly what direction the case will take. However, the investigators should be guided by certain basic procedures at the scene.

- ☐ Ascertain that there is an investigator at the scene and that the crime scene is amply protected. Confer with the initial investigator and get up to date on the status of the investigation. Solicit any opinions or theories, and objectively evaluate these with your independent observations. Determine any investigative needs, and make assignments as necessary.

- ☐ Confer with the ranking uniformed officer at the scene, and interview the first officer so that proper instructions can be given to responding investigators.

- ☐ Priority should be given to the removal of the suspect and/or witnesses to the police station. Each witness should be transported separately. However, before they are transported, the witnesses should be briefly interviewed by the investigators at the scene so that they may have the advantage of the witnesses' observations to guide their investigation at the scene. Written statements can be obtained later at the police station and the information transmitted to the detective supervisor at the scene.

- ☐ Use an assignment sheet to indicate assignments given. This sheet should contain the identification of officers assigned, the location of the assignment, the duties assigned, and the time the assignment was given. Later, it can be used as a control device to assure that official reports are obtained from the investigators assigned. In addition to fixing responsibility for certain investigative duties, the assignment sheet will eliminate duplication of effort as additional assignments are made and entered on the sheet.

☐ If a suitable communications center or command post has not been established by the patrol officers, the investigator or supervisor should take immediate steps to arrange for one. The station house, Communications Division, and detective command should be apprised of the telephone numbers and/or cellular numbers utilized at the command post to facilitate rapid communication to and from the scene.

☐ Designate an officer to keep a running timetable of events, including arrivals and departures at the scene. When the scene is released, the timetable should be turned over to the detective supervisor.

☐ If the victim has been removed to a hospital, ensure that proper action is being taken at the hospital regarding any dying declarations, clothing, evidence, etc. It is advisable to have a detective contact the hospital and confer with the patrol officer and/or doctor. It may even be necessary to assign a detective to assist the officer in these procedures.

☐ If the suspect has fled the scene, the investigator and detective supervisor must ascertain exactly what alarms have been transmitted, if any, and the exact information contained therein. Upon verification and the development of any new information, these alarms should be retransmitted. Broadcast alarms or "Be on the Lookout" alerts (BOLOs) periodically on *ALL* watches until no longer needed. Cancel alarms when no longer pertinent.

☐ Expand BOLOs to include the entire state, nation, and border crossings, if needed.

☐ Use license plate reader services, the National Law Enforcement Telecommunications System (NLETS), and the National Crime Information Center (NCIC).

☐ Provide for the dissemination of information to all units involved in the homicide investigation. Ideally, all investigators should be aware of all aspects of the case.

It is up to the detective supervisor to coordinate and disseminate this information to the "troops." Properly informed officers can better perform their own assigned functions and contribute more intelligently to the overall effort. This is especially true for those officers assigned to conduct canvasses. Uniformed officers assisting at the scene must also be made to feel that they are part of the team. On occasion, too many officers may respond to the homicide crime scene. The detective supervisor should not hesitate to direct these officers to return to their original assignments if they are not needed.

Specific Investigative Duties at the Scene

The Suspect in Custody

When the suspect has been taken into custody by patrol officers, the immediate responsibilities of the detectives or homicide investigators should be the following:

- ☐ Ensure that the suspect has been removed from, or is not allowed to enter, the primary crime scene. The isolation of the suspect is necessary in order to prevent scene contamination or destruction of evidence.
- ☐ Interview the arresting officer(s), out of the hearing of the suspect, in order to determine the scope of the initial investigation, the location of any physical evidence, and the probable cause for the arrest of the suspect, including any statements made by the suspect or witnesses.
- ☐ Instruct these officers, upon completion of this preliminary interview, to document in writing their observations and activities at the scene, including any overhears or statements made by the suspect, as well as any information provided by witnesses or informants.
- ☐ Ascertain whether or not the suspect has been given his or her Miranda warning by the patrol officers, to assure the admissibility of any culpable statements made to these officers. Never assume that a Miranda warning has been given. Ensure that you provide the suspect with his or her Miranda rights, and document this.

Miranda Warning

1. You have the right to remain silent.
2. Anything you say can and will be used against you in a court of law.
3. You have the right to talk to a lawyer and have him present with you while you are being questioned.
4. If you cannot afford to hire a lawyer, one will be appointed to represent you before any questioning, if you wish one.

Waiver

After the warning and in order to secure a waiver, the following questions should be asked and an affirmative reply secured to each question.

1. Do you understand each of these rights I have explained to you?
2. Having these rights in mind, do you wish to talk to us now?

Evaluation of the Suspect's Demeanor and Mental Capacity

This observation and documentation are necessary to prepare against a possible diminished capacity defense, which is usually based on the contention that the defendant, at the time that the offense was committed, was not able to determine right or wrong. The defense of diminished capacity is a popular one because the police often fail to take proper precautions during the initial investigation.

The following are some important observations that should be recorded in the investigator's notebook:

- ☐ Does the suspect speak rationally or irrationally?
- ☐ Does he or she answer in a straightforward or evasive manner?
- ☐ Is the response to questioning intelligent or confused?
- ☐ Does the suspect have control over his or her actions?
- ☐ What is the suspect's emotional condition?
- ☐ Is there any evidence of intoxication, or does the suspect appear to be under the influence of any drugs or alcohol?
- ☐ Does the suspect give any reasons for his or her actions?
- ☐ When investigators interview witnesses, they should attempt to obtain as much information as possible regarding the actions of the

suspect prior to the crime, during the crime, and immediately after the crime. Any indications of the suspect's demeanor and mental capacity should be recorded.
- ☐ The witnesses should be asked the following questions:
  - ☐ What was the suspect's appearance at the time of the crime?
  - ☐ How did the suspect act?
  - ☐ Could the witness determine the suspect's demeanor or mental state?
  - ☐ Did the suspect act rationally or irrationally?
  - ☐ Was the act a cold-blooded or unemotional thing?
  - ☐ Did the suspect scream or yell?
  - ☐ How did the suspect commit the act?
  - ☐ Did the suspect say or do anything during or after the crime?
  - ☐ Did the suspect attempt to flee or cover up the crime?

Obtaining a Dying Declaration

If the victim is still alive when investigators arrive at the scene, they should attempt to obtain a statement. Likewise, if a victim has been removed to a hospital, detectives should immediately be dispatched so that they may interview him or her.

In cases where the victim is seriously injured and death will undoubtedly occur, investigators must be alert to the possibility of obtaining a dying declaration. This can be obtained while waiting for the ambulance, en route to the hospital, or while the victim is in the hospital. As long as investigators do not interfere with life-sustaining measures or hinder medical personnel by their presence, there should be no problems.

The dying declaration may prove invaluable in firmly establishing whether or not a crime has occurred, and, more importantly, who was responsible. In order to obtain a legally admissible declaration, however, certain conditions must exist. They are as follows:

- ☐ The victim must believe that he or she is going to die.
- ☐ The victim must have no hope of recovery.

☐ The declaration or statement must refer to
  1. The manner and circumstances which brought about the victim's condition and ultimate death
  2. The identity of the person responsible
☐ The declarant must die.
☐ The declarant must have been otherwise competent and rational.

Questions to Be Asked in a Dying Declaration

There are no set guidelines for the exact sequence of questions one should ask when attempting to obtain a dying declaration. Basically, you will want to establish through your questions that the witness is competent, is lucid, and does believe that he or she is about to die. Here are some questions that the investigator may find helpful:

☐ What is your name?
☐ Where do you live?
☐ Do you now believe that you are about to die?
☐ Have you any hope of recovery?
☐ Are you willing to make a true statement of how and why you were injured?

Documentation of the Dying Declaration

The statement can be either oral or, if feasible, written by the declarant. Ideally, the investigator will have the ability to record the statement during this event. In any case, the officer should reduce the statement to writing and have the declarant either sign it or make his or her mark. It is recommended that there be a civilian witness present; however, the fact that there was no witness available or that the declarant was unable to write or sign the statement does not affect the admissibility of the declaration in court.

Suicide Investigation

The rationale behind suicide, which is defined as the intentional taking of one's own life, can be simple or as complex as life itself. The person who commits suicide may see his or her actions as some sort of solution to a severe physical or psychological dilemma. Oftentimes, a police investigator will find a note indicating that the victim had suffered psychological torment or was severely depressed. The note might even suggest that he or she believed that suicide was the last resort. Many of the suicide notes I have seen over the years indicate the acute depression of persons who have taken their lives. Depression does not discriminate. It affects the young and old alike.

Investigatively speaking, all death investigations should be handled as homicide cases until the facts prove differently.

The resolution of the mode of death as suicide is based on a series of factors that eliminate homicide, accidents, and natural causes of death.

>**Remember: Do it right the first time. You only get one chance.**

Three Investigative Considerations in Determining the Manner of Death (Homicide or Suicide)

The investigator should be aware of three basic considerations to establish if a death is suicidal in nature.

- [ ] The presence of the weapon or means of death at the scene
- [ ] Injuries or wounds that are obviously self-inflicted or could have been inflicted by the deceased
- [ ] The existence of a motive on the part of the deceased to take his or her own life

Suicide Notes

The presence of a suicide note certainly suggests suicide. However, the investigator should conduct a further inquiry to ascertain whether the note is genuine.

- [ ] Was it written by the deceased?
- [ ] Was it written voluntarily?

☐ Collect the note in a manner that will preserve any latent fingerprints.
☐ Obtain a sample of known writings of the deceased (exemplars) for comparison.
☐ The note oftentimes provides a basis of inquiry into the background of the victim.
☐ Examine computers and cell phones for incoming and outgoing text messages.
☐ Identify and interview recipients of text or e-mail messages.

Suicide Checklist

Important note: Most suicides occur as a result of depression. Therefore, the investigator should concentrate part of the inquiry into the clinical component of the event. However, keep in mind that some suicides are conscious decisions on the part of the victim and the particular motive for the event may never be ascertained.

Investigative Considerations

The manner of death may be important in determining suicidal intent. People who shoot or hang themselves or jump to their deaths certainly have indicated an intention to take their lives. Suicide by hanging is extremely common. In fact, following firearms, it is the most popular method of suicide. *Similarly, deaths involving a combination of methods (poisoning, shooting, slashing of wrists, inhaling gas, etc.) show an extreme desire to die.*

See Figure 5 for examples of suspension by hanging.

Remember: **Almost all hangings are suicidal.**

Exceptions: **Accidental deaths due to asphyxia by hanging (e.g., autoerotic fatalities) and homicides made to look like suicide (e.g., "staged crime scenes").**

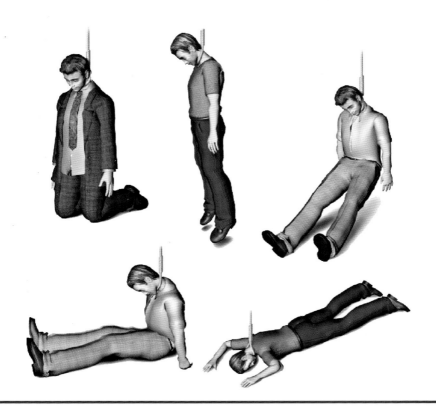

FIGURE 5 *There can be complete or incomplete suspension* in cases involving hanging. (Illustration courtesy of Brian Wilson, Medical Legal Art, © 2010, www.doereport.com.)

Evaluation of the Wounds

☐ Could the deceased have caused the injuries and death?
☐ Was the person physically able to accomplish the act?
☐ Are the wounds within reach of the deceased?
☐ Are the wounds grouped together?
☐ Is there more than one cause of death?
☐ Describe the nature and position of the injuries.
☐ Evaluate the lethality of the wounds.

☐ Does it appear that the subject was intent on killing him or herself (e.g., overkill such as jumping from a tall building versus a low building, or taking a lot of pills versus a few)?

☐ Are there any hesitation marks?

Weapons or Means of Death

☐ The weapon or means of death should be present in cases of suicide. However, the absence of a weapon does not necessarily indicate that the death was due to a homicide. The weapon or means of death could have been disposed of prior to the arrival of the authorities, or family members may have removed items from the scene.

☐ Weapons commonly associated with suicides are handguns and long-barrel rifles.

☐ Intraoral gunshot wounds, as well as contact wounds to the temple and beneath the chin, are most commonly suicides.

☐ As a general rule, suicidal gunshot wounds are almost always contact wounds.

☐ Most *contact shotgun wounds* of the head are *suicidal in origin*.

☐ Suicidal gunshot wounds are usually fired by the dominant hand.

☐ If the weapon is in the hands of the victim, examine the hands for the presence of cadaveric spasm (instantaneous rigor mortis).

☐ Examine the hands for the presence of any soot or gunpowder residue.

☐ The weapon should be examined for evidence of discharge and operability.

☐ The weapon should be examined for the presence of any blowback materials, including blood from the victim.

☐ Suicide by hanging is extremely common. Following firearms, hangings are the most popular method of suicide.

☐ Collect any ligatures and/or ropes.

☐ Suicide by stabbing or cutting usually results in the presence of "hesitation wounds." Exception would be persons who are psychotic or under the influence of drugs or alcohol.

☐ Collect the sharp-edged instruments for the presence of any fingerprints.

☐ Suicide by overdose is also popular. Collect any medications, drugs, or pharmaceuticals.
☐ Suicide by helium is also a popular choice for suicides.

Psychological Aspects

Warning Signs in Suicide

☐ A change in sleeping habits—sleeping more than usual or staying up much later, followed by sadness
☐ A change in eating habits—weight loss or lack of appetite
☐ A lack of interest in sex—loss of sex drive
☐ A sudden drop in grades or school attendance (young people), or loss of work interest (adults)
☐ Loss of interest in favorite activities, hobbies, or sports
☐ Isolation: loss of interest in friends, family, etc.
☐ A preoccupation with death, or an unusual interest in art or music dealing with death (e.g., in teenagers, heavy metal, rock; in adults, a preoccupation with death and the afterlife)
☐ Loss of interest in personal hygiene and appearance
☐ Involvement with drugs, including alcohol

Extreme Danger Signs

☐ Suddenly becoming cheerful or calm after a depression—a sudden euphoria or burst of activity. This could mean that the person has resolved the inner conflict by deciding to take his or her life. The decision is made.
☐ Giving away prized possessions
☐ Speaking of life in the past tense, e.g., saying, "I've loved you," or "You've been a good mother"

Psychological State of the Victim

☐ Obtain a background of the victim from family and friends. This background should include medical as well as social information.
☐ Were there any *warning signs* indicated by the victim?
☐ Were there any recent deaths in the family?

☐ Is there any indication of a recent upset or stress?
☐ Did the victim leave any notes? Request a sample of the victim's handwriting for analysis in case a note is later discovered.
☐ Any close personal relationships, close friends, etc.? Interview as soon as possible.

Spite Suicides

☐ Suicides where the person committing the act wants to punish or shock the survivors are not uncommon. Such suicides may kill themselves inside the home or at the workplace, where a suicide by a long-barreled firearm will create an extremely bloody mess or scene.
☐ The person who decides to commit suicide may have a lot of anger, and there is a very thin line between homicide and suicide.

> *Remember*: **A person who is willing to commit suicide is very capable of killing another person. Family annihilations are examples of this extreme anger and rage.**

Any Prior Mental Disease or Defect

☐ Has the deceased been under any professional treatment?
☐ Had the deceased ever attempted suicide in the past?
☐ Has anyone in the family ever committed suicide? (Who, when, why, and how?)
☐ Was the deceased a heavy drinker?
☐ Was the deceased on any medication? Include prescribed psychotropic drugs, sleep aids, and over-the-counter medications.
☐ If so, what was the dosage amount prescribed? Amount left in bottle? Prescribing doctor or facility?
☐ Was there a history of drug abuse?
☐ Was there a history of physical or psychological abuse to the deceased?

Consider a Psychological Autopsy

The psychological autopsy is a collaborative procedure involving law enforcement and mental health experts who attempt to determine what the state of mind of a person was prior to the fatal act.

Conduct a victimology and examine the victim's lifestyle, and interview the victim's friends and relatives to determine whether the death was accidental or involved suicide.

Final Exit Suicides

Final Exit–type suicides are distinctively unique from other suicide cases. They are planned events with the possibility of victim assistance. Law enforcement personnel who investigate sudden and violent deaths have a responsibility to properly document and classify these events.

Investigative Checklist for Final Exit Cases

- ☐ Is the book *Final Exit* by Derek Humphry (New York: Dell, 1992) at the crime scene?
  - ☐ Check the book for any entries, highlighting, or writing relative to what is observed in the crime scene or any evidence of "acts of self-deliverance."
- ☐ Are there any suicide notes at the scene? If so, seize these notes as evidence for fingerprint and handwriting analysis.
- ☐ Obtain a handwriting exemplar (writings of the deceased when he or she was still alive).
- ☐ Examine computers and smartphones for suicide-related websites.
- ☐ Compare the contents of any notes with the "Letters to Be Written" chapter in the book *Final Exit*.
- ☐ Take "major-case" prints of the deceased. These include not only fingerprints, but palmar (hand) prints as well.
- ☐ Request major-case prints from all persons present or who are considered close to the deceased.

The Plastic Bag

The presence of a plastic bag at the scene is highly suggestive of *Final Exit*–type suicides. The investigator should note and document the following:

- ☐ Is there a plastic bag over the victim's head or present at the crime scene?

- [ ] Submit the entire plastic bag for an examination of latent finger-prints. Check the plastic bag for any fingerprints for comparison or elimination with the deceased.
- [ ] Seize all prescription drugs or medications at the scene for subsequent toxicological examination.
- [ ] Note drug names, doctor, pharmacist, and date.
- [ ] Compare these with the drug dosage chart in *Final Exit*.

Remember: **There is a presumption of possible victim assistance in these types of suicides based upon the information in *Final Exit*.**

Suicide-by-Cop Scenarios

The term *suicide by cop* is a police colloquialism used to describe incidents in which individuals, bent on self-destruction, engage in life-threatening and criminal behavior in order to force the police to kill them.

Some Suicide Indicators

- [ ] The subject sets a deadline for his or her own death.
- [ ] Mentioning names of people who are dead and talking about them as if they are still alive or indicating that he or she will soon be with them.
- [ ] Making verbal statements or arrangements for the disposition of "worldly goods"; giving away "prized possessions," which include items he or she has at the time of the negotiations (e.g., wristwatch or jewelry).
- [ ] Subject may create a confrontational face-to-face negotiating posture with the police.
- [ ] Making an announcement or declaration of an intent to die.
- [ ] Making biblical references, specifically as they relate to the Book of Revelations and resurrection.

Autoerotic Fatalities

Investigative Considerations

- [ ] Sex-related deaths due to solo sex-related activities, which usually involve asphyxia, are generally defined as autoerotic fatalities.
- [ ] In most instances, the mechanism of death is asphyxia by hanging, ligature, plastic bags, or chemical substances.
- [ ] Atypical asphyxiation-related methods, such as chest compression, smothering, and immersion or drowning, may be employed as well as electrocution, foreign body insertion, and other miscellaneous methodologies causing some other physiological derangement which results in death.
- [ ] The manner of death, based on first observation, may be classified as either suicide or homicide, when in fact it is actually an accident that occurred during a dangerous autoerotic act.
- [ ] The speed of death in hangings is as follows:
    - [ ] Rapid loss of consciousness occurs between 8 and 18 seconds.
    - [ ] Closely followed by convulsions at 10–19 seconds
    - [ ] Followed by a complex pattern of decerebrate and decorticate rigidity.
- [ ] The following pattern of bruises is usual and nonsuspicious in hanging:
    - [ ] Bruises on the posterior part of arms, on the anterior part of legs, and on either arms or legs
    - [ ] To find bruises on the anterior part of arms, the posterior part of legs, or both arms and legs is suspicious and requires further investigation.
    - [ ] Most victims of autoerotic fatality will be discovered in secluded areas of the home or workplace during nonbusiness hours (attics, basements, garages, bathrooms, or bedrooms).
- [ ] Outdoor locations are usually secluded areas.
- [ ] Look for the presence of any digital or recording devices.

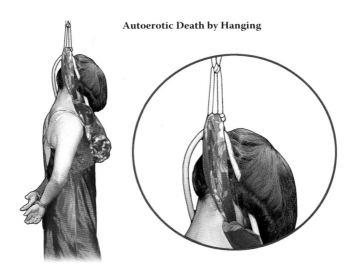

Autoerotic Death by Hanging

FIGURE 6 Typical autoerotic death. This victim was discovered in a full hang, suspended by the neck with an electrical cord secured to a rafter in the ceiling. He was wearing a full-length pink dress and high-heeled shoes and had apparently slipped from the chair as he attempted to stop hanging. Note the padding between the noose and the neck of the victim. Case example submitted by Detective J. J. Mead, Columbus (Ohio) Police Department. Graphic courtesy of Brian Wilson, Medical Legal Art, © 2012, www.doereport.com. Submitted from files of Vernon Geberth.

- ☐ Check for any obvious changes in the crime scene (body redressed, erotic materials, and/or sexual paraphernalia removed).
- ☐ Interview emergency medical services (EMS) personnel or ambulance personnel who may have arrived before the police to ascertain their observations.
- ☐ Interview family members for background information on the victim.
- ☐ Were there any prior incidents involving these activities?

Figure 6 depicts a typical autoerotic death.

Autoerotic Checklist: Determining the Involvement of Sexual Asphyxia

There are certain questions which the investigator should consider in determining whether or not the death is related to autoerotic activity.

- ☐ Is the victim nude, sexually exposed, or—if a male—dressed in articles of feminine attire: transvestitism, makeup, and/or wigs?
- ☐ Is there evidence of masturbatory activity: tissues, towels, or hanky in hand, or in shorts to catch semen? Seminal fluids?
- ☐ Is there evidence of infibulations: piercing or causing pain to the genitalia, self-torture, masochism, pins in penis, etc.?
- ☐ Are sexually stimulating paraphernalia present: vibrators, dildos, sex aids, pornographic magazines, butt plugs, etc.?
- ☐ Is bondage present: ropes, chains, blindfolds, gags, etc.? Are any constrictive devices present: corsets, plastic wrap, belts, ropes, vacuum cleaner hoses around the body, or chest constraints?
- ☐ Is there protective padding between the ligature and the neck: towels, rags, or cloth, to prevent rope burns or discomfort?
- ☐ Are the restraints interconnected? Do the ropes and ties come together, or are they connected? Are the chains interconnected through one another? Is the victim tied to himself, so that by putting pressure on one of the limbs the restraints are tightened?
- ☐ Are mirrors or other reflective devices present? Are they positioned so that the victim can view his or her activities?
- ☐ Is there evidence of fantasy (diaries, erotic literature, etc.) or fetishism (woman's panties, bras, girdles, leather, rubber, latex, high-heeled shoes, etc.)?
- ☐ Is the suspension point within reach of the victim, or is there an escape mechanism (keys, lock, slip knot, etc.)?
- ☐ Is there evidence of prior such activities (abrasions or rope burns on suspension point; unexplained secretive behavior, or long stays in isolated areas; rope burns on neck, etc.)?
- ☐ Does the victim possess literature dealing with bondage, escapology, or knots?
- ☐ Is there a positioned camera? (Check film and/or videotapes. Look for photos, and view any videotapes in camera.)

While not all such deaths will involve the above characteristics, their presence will certainly alert the investigator to the possibility of death occurring as the result of sexual misadventure.

Investigating Fatal Fires Checklist

Investigative Considerations

- ☐ Was the fire intentional or accidental?
- ☐ Was the victim alive or dead before the fire?
  - ☐ Many times arson is used to conceal a homicide, disguise a crime scene, or destroy evidence.

The Fire Incident

- ☐ Identify the fire officer in charge of fire operations. Obtain the name, rank, assignment, and unit responsibility of all fire personnel involved in the operation.
- ☐ Obtain a copy of the chief's report describing the fire department's operations taken to extinguish the fire: This includes
  - ☐ Determination of origin/cause—suspicious or otherwise.
  - ☐ Was the fire incendiary? What accelerant was used?

Suspicious Designation: General Determination Factors

- ☐ Rate of burning not consistent with type of combustibles present in the location at the time of fire.
- ☐ A person died as a result of the fire.
- ☐ Questionable or multiple points of origin of the fire.
- ☐ Firefighter(s) noticed odor of gasoline or other accelerant.
- ☐ Cause not readily determined.

Maintenance of the Fire Crime Scene

Determine the condition of the scene based upon the fire department's operations (body moved, debris removed, building collapse, etc.).

Investigation at the Scene

- ☐ Interview survivors as soon as possible.
- ☐ Interview people with an interest in the fire who may still be present at the scene while firefighters are working.

- [ ] Interview firefighters who have firsthand knowledge of the conditions within the building.
- [ ] Obtain information on all injured, evacuated, and relocated persons for interview.
- [ ] Interview any ambulance, paramedic, or other emergency crews, including Red Cross personnel who assisted with operations.
- [ ] Initiate an investigative canvass (see "Initiate a Canvass").
- [ ] Covertly photograph onlookers and bystanders, if possible.
- [ ] Note the license plates of vehicles that have scanner antennae visible.
- [ ] Assign a fire investigator or arson expert to begin an origin/cause investigation at the scene to make an official determination of the fire incident.
- [ ] Record the crime scene—conduct the crime scene search.
- [ ] Examine the body.
  - [ ] Investigative considerations in arson cases:
    - [ ] Identity of the victim
    - [ ] Was victim dead or alive?
    - [ ] Is victim face-up or face-down (usually when people collapse, they fall face-forward)?
    - [ ] Does the body evince a "pugilistic attitude": a boxing pose or fetal position caused by the effect of heat upon the muscles?
    - [ ] Postmortem lividity should be pink to cherry red due to the inhalation of carbon monoxide if the person was alive and breathing during the fire.
    - [ ] Is there blistering: Blisters surrounded by a pink ring can be considered as having occurred before death. However, the medical examiner makes the final call.

Determination of Arson

The determination of arson must be based upon expert opinion. This opinion is established after a careful review of the facts based on the ability of the expert to "read the fire," which provides the investigator with the necessary legal basis for an arson determination and subsequent prosecution.

Sudden Infant Death Syndrome (SIDS)

Note: Investigators should be aware that some deaths that appear to be SIDS deaths may in fact turn out to be homicides. These homicides may be due to smothering or Munchausen syndrome by proxy (MSBP) cases. In other cases, the injuries may be internal, and an external examination of the child fails to reveal any trauma. For further information, see SUID-SIDS Resource Center (www.sidscenter.org).

Investigative Checklist

- [ ] Infant's pedigree
  - [ ] Age, date of birth, sex, race, birth weight
  - [ ] Location of birth
  - [ ] Natural delivery or Caesarian section?
  - [ ] Full-term or premature birth?
  - [ ] Complications?
  - [ ] Length of hospital stay
- [ ] Date and time when the death was discovered
  - [ ] Who was the last person to see the child alive? Date and time.
  - [ ] Who discovered the dead infant? Date and time.
- [ ] What was the place of death?
  - [ ] Child's crib, bed, parent's bed, other location? Describe.
- [ ] Position of the infant/child when found dead?
  - [ ] Had this original position been changed? By whom? And why?
- [ ] Was resuscitation attempted?
  - [ ] Name of person who attempted resuscitation
  - [ ] Method of resuscitation
- [ ] Had the infant/child been sick lately?
  - [ ] Cold or sniffles?
  - [ ] Other minor or major illnesses?
- [ ] Any medical treatment? What treatment prescribed?
  - [ ] Seeing a doctor? Treating physician?
  - [ ] Any medication? What type? Name and dosage?

- [ ] Was the infant/child breast-fed Or bottle-fed?
    - [ ] When was the time of last feeding?
    - [ ] What was fed to the infant/child?
    - [ ] Send baby bottle of the formula given to the baby to either the medical examiner's office or crime lab.
    - [ ] Recover unused powder formula or ready-made formula.
    - [ ] Document lot numbers.
- [ ] Have the parents noticed any difference in the infant's/child's appearance or behavior in the last few days?
- [ ] When was the baby last examined by a physician? Why, and by whom?
- [ ] Was the baby exposed to any illnesses recently?
- [ ] Had there been illness in the family recently?
- [ ] Have there been any other SIDS deaths in the family? If yes, take a complete history.
- [ ] Has the family lived in other states and/or countries? Identify where. Cross-check using online services (e.g., LexisNexis).
- [ ] Was someone other than the parent caring for infant/child? Obtain name, address, etc.
    - [ ] Ascertain whether any other infants or children have died under their care.

Munchausen Syndrome by Proxy

Warning Signs

- [ ] MSBP is characterized by illness which is unexplained, prolonged, and so extraordinary that experienced doctors state they have never seen anything like it.
- [ ] Repeat hospitalizations and extensive medical tests without achieving a diagnosis
- [ ] Symptoms and signs that do not make medical sense
- [ ] Persistent failure of the victim to respond to therapy
- [ ] Signs and symptoms that dissipate when the victim is removed from the suspected offender

- [ ] Mothers who do not seem worried about their children's illnesses and are constantly at the child's side while in the hospital
- [ ] Mothers who have an unusually close relationship with the medical staff
- [ ] Families who have had other children labeled as SIDS deaths
- [ ] Mothers with previous medical or nursing experience who often give a history of the same type of illness as the child
- [ ] A parent who welcomes medical testing of the child, even if painful
- [ ] A parent who attempts to convince the staff that the child is still ill, when advised that the child will be released from the hospital
- [ ] A "model family" who normally would be above suspicion
- [ ] A caretaker with a previous history of Munchausen syndrome
- [ ] A caretaker who adamantly refuses to accept the suggestion that the diagnosis is nonmedical

Crime Scene Documentation

Documentation of Crime Scene Photographs

The number of photos taken is usually determined by the case. There is no limit on the number that can be taken. Practically speaking, it is always better to overshoot a scene than to miss some vital shots.

As each photo is taken, an accurate record should be made in the investigator's notebook. In addition, an entry should be made on an official photo log. Some agencies maintain logs or preprinted forms for use at crime scenes in order to assure the proper documentation of crime scene photographs. In any event, the following information should be recorded:

- [ ] The date and time
- [ ] The exact location
- [ ] The case number
- [ ] A brief description of the detail being photographed
- [ ] The compass direction (north, south, east, or west)
- [ ] The type of film and camera utilized
- [ ] Any special equipment utilized

- [ ] Lighting and weather conditions
- [ ] The number of exposures
- [ ] The identity of the photographer
- [ ] The location of the exposed film or media storage cards
- [ ] The digital file size and format: JPEG, TIFF, or NEF

The photographer should keep possession of the exposed film for delivery to the laboratory for processing. After these photos are developed, the above information should be entered either on the back of each photo or on an appropriate form indicating each photo by number.

- [ ] Photographs should be taken at the highest resolution available to the camera being used. Copies of the crime scene images can be reduced in size at a later date using readily available software, should they need to be electronically transmitted via the Internet.
- [ ] Although a tripod is not always practical or manageable, it should be used to support the camera. It acts to stabilize the camera, and provides a consistent height of the camera when moved about the crime scene.
- [ ] The use of a tripod is a must when photographing scenes in poor lighting conditions.
- [ ] Most digital cameras provide for a completely automatic operation. The photographer need only compose the image and take the photo.
- [ ] Not all scene and lighting conditions will lend themselves to a camera with completely automatic operations. The photographer should familiarize him or herself with the manual-override feature of the camera prior to its use in the field.
- [ ] The convenience of digital photography is that the photographer will instantly be made aware if a usable photograph has been rendered or not.
- [ ] The photographer should never delete any image from the storage or memory card. Images recorded onto the memory card are recorded with sequential identifying file names and the time and date on which the images were produced, provided the correct time and date are set on the camera. Any missing images on a memory card

will be cause for concern of any defense attorney at trial. Some cameras will also record the exposure settings, lens focal length, and longitude and latitude location of where the image was taken.

☐ If test shots are made, they should be noted as such on the photo log and not deleted.

Recommended Crime Scene Photographs

☐ The photographer should begin by taking an overall or establishing photograph of the crime scene. Note the lens used or the focal-length setting if a zoom lens is used. The scene should be free of any personnel or equipment brought with them.

☐ If the crime scene is located outside, the first overall or establishing photograph should always be orientated to the north, with overall photos then being taken at each of the remaining compass points: east, south, and west.

☐ If necessary, photograph the route, path, or road needed to access the crime scene. Utilize aerial photography if practical.

☐ Crime scene markers with compass point designations should be introduced only after photographs are taken without their use.

☐ Only after the scene has been completely photographed should the inclusion of markers, flags, rulers, or scales be introduced and photographed.

☐ If the crime scene is located inside a building or structure, the first overall or establishing photograph should incorporate the building or structure orientated to the north, with overall photos then being taken at each of the remaining compass points: east, south, and west.

☐ The front of the building or structure should be photographed next and a progression of photographs taken along the route to enter the actual crime scene itself.

1. Photographs should be taken showing the condition of the doorway and door, both inside and out. Pay special attention to any identifying marks such as apartment or suite numbers.

2. Once inside the doorway, take an establishing photograph as to just how the room looks upon entering it. Enter and move in a

clockwise manner, photographing the room from each of the four corners.

3. Photograph the room using medium points of view and move in a clockwise manner, taking photographs from each of the four compass points.

4. Close-up photography of evidence as well as evidence *in situ* should be performed next. Establish shots of evidence in relationship to other distinguishable parts of the crime scene.

5. Photograph the ceiling. This can best be accomplished by placing the camera on the floor, facing the ceiling, and activating the self-timer function or enlisting the aid of a wireless remote control if the camera has such a function. Activate the self-timer, and leave the room until the exposure has been completed.

6. Ensure that all areas of the ceiling have been covered.

7. Photograph the floor.

☐ Proceed to the next room if necessary, and repeat steps 1–7.

☐ Only after the scene has been completely photographed should the inclusion of markers, flags, rulers, or scales be introduced and photographed. The scene should be photographed in the same sequence.

☐ Once work at the crime scene is completely finished, exit photographs should be taken to document in what condition the scene was left. If the scene is to be locked or sealed with the aid of some type of evidence tape or medical examiner's/coroner's seal, the tape should be photographed.

☐ A close-up shot of any identifying signature, times, or dates should be taken. If (or when) investigators need to return to the crime scene, photographs of the seals and/or tape showing their condition should be taken.

Photographs of Deceased Subjects

☐ The deceased subject should be incorporated throughout the crime scene photographs, but should also be subject to a separate, thorough photographic documentation.

☐ Ideally, the first photograph should be an identifying facial image. This may not be practical if the remains are face-down. If this is the case, then the identifying facial image can be taken when the remains are rolled over.

☐ Start at the head of the remains, and work downward toward the feet. Employ medium point-of-view photographs.

☐ Gently open the eyelids, and photograph the eyes for the presence or absence of *petechial hemorrhage*. A short telephoto lens or a macro lens is ideal for this type of image.

☐ Document any injuries or evidence with a close-up image.

☐ Continue until you arrive at the feet.

☐ Roll over the subject onto its back if found face-up or onto its front if found face-down.

☐ Repeat the steps starting from the head down to the feet.

☐ Reposition the body to either side, and photograph anything that may have been missed on the prior passes.

☐ Only after the remains have been completely photographed should the inclusion of markers, rulers, or scales be introduced and photographed. The remains should be photographed in the same sequence.

☐ An ABFO #2 scale should be utilized when photographing gunshot wounds, sharp-force injuries, or bite marks.

☐ Photograph the area underneath the subject once the body is removed from the scene.

☐ The subject should be rephotographed in the same manner after it arrives at the medical examiner's /coroner's facility and is undressed and made ready for autopsy.

Videotape Protocol

Arrival at Scene

☐ Obtain the preliminary information from the first personnel on the scene regarding the occurrence: any observations by witnesses who have entered the crime scene, any EMS activities, etc. Check with the investigators, medical examiners, etc. regarding what they think.

☐ The technician, at this point, should quickly take a look at the scene for such things as

A. Location
   1. Layout of the apartment
   2. The room the body is in and other rooms where evidence is found
   3. Areas that you should be careful not to disturb, such as blood on the floors or walls, small pieces of evidence that could easily be kicked or stepped on. *Use your elbows to open doors instead of imparting your fingerprints or handprints in the crime scene.*

B. Body
   1. Size of the room in which it was found
   2. Whether face-up or face-down, and accessible from what angles?
   3. The wounds: how many, where, and what kind?

Taping Protocol Checklist

☐ Begin taping by putting an introduction on the tape: technician's name, date, time, and location.

☐ Turn off the audio. You do not want to have an ongoing commentary regarding the scene. Opinions and perspectives change.

Remember: The tape is subject to discovery. You do not want to pick up stray comments or information on the open microphone. Later on in court, the witness can narrate.

☐ Begin taping from a logical beginning point, e.g., front door, nearest identifiable landmark, or (if outdoors) a street sign.

☐ Orientate your camera work so that viewers will know where you are at a given point; e.g., pan the room or hallway before being specific. Go slowly and use long steady shots.

☐ Shoot the scene from a normal angle as the eye would perceive it without wide-angle or telescopic distortion.

☐ When you do zoom in, zoom back out to the same spot. This will provide the viewer continuity and perspective, and allow editing of zoom proportions. Never zoom without purpose. *The single most overused and abused feature of the novice recorder is the zoom.*

☐ When zooming in, sharpen focus and hold.

☐ Do not do each item on a separate zoom (e.g., in and out on each bullet wound). A much more effective tape will be procured when you zoom to a series of small items or wounds, pan across them slowly, and then zoom out very slowly.

☐ Shoot several angles of the body, room, etc. Try to shoot the body from adjoining rooms if possible or down long hallways. This provides the possible lines of sight that still photos can't depict.

☐ Shoot all doors, locks, windows, closets, kitchen, dining facilities, medicine cabinets, etc.

☐ Shoot all lines of sight at location (e.g., top of stairs to downstairs front door and in reverse).

☐ Shoot the body at the end of the scene documentation.

☐ After the body has been turned over, reshoot those areas which were hidden from view to document any further wounds or findings.

☐ Shoot hands, feet, eyes, clothes, jewelry, tattoos, gold teeth, scars, etc.

☐ *Optional*: Shoot the recovery and collection of evidence.

☐ Shoot all bloodstains, weapons, shell casings, hair, fibers, and trace evidence.

☐ Upon completion of the taping, close with your name and time.

☐ Label and number tape, and log as evidence; include weather conditions, lighting, etc.

Remember: **Videotaping does not replace good crime scene photographs. It should be used in conjunction with the photos.**

Documentation of the Crime Scene Sketch

The Title Block

The professional and legally correct crime scene sketch must contain the following official documentation and information:

☐ The name and title of the investigator who drew the sketch
☐ The date and time when the sketch was made

☐ The classification of the crime (homicide, assault, etc.)
☐ The identification of the victim
☐ The agency's case number
☐ The names of any persons assisting in taking measurements
☐ The precise address of the location sketched
☐ Reference points during the sketching, including compass direction north, with appropriate indications
☐ *The legend*: The purpose of the legend is to identify every article or object by either number or letter, and explain the significance of these characters on the crime scene sketch. The legend also includes the scale used and a reference to any notes taken and measurements recorded in connection with the investigation.
☐ Any other pertinent information which is practical to the investigation at the scene, such as the season, the ground condition (e.g., muddy, dry), traffic or lack of traffic, slope of the ground, site (e.g., abandoned building, public place, transportation facility), the position of the camera in any crime scene photographs

It is important to note that any number of crime scene sketches may be employed during the investigation at the scene, especially in multiple crime scene situations. Therefore, it is imperative that any sketch used be properly documented in the investigator's notebook along with descriptions and other pertinent information. Figure 7 gives an example of a cross-projection sketch, and Figure 8 shows the baseline method of sketching. Figure 9 pertains to the crime scene search and when to obtain a warrant.

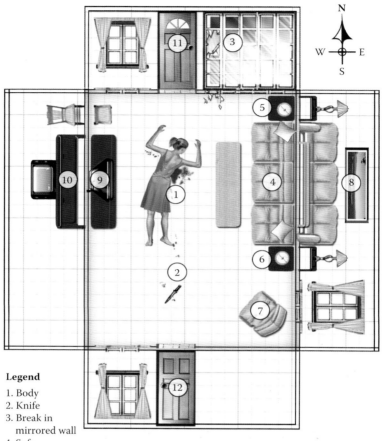

Legend

1. Body
2. Knife
3. Break in
   mirrored wall
4. Sofa
5. & 6. End tables
7. Chair
8. Framed photograph
9. T.V.
10. Cabinet
11. Front door
12. Back door

Homicide: #1234/05 October 29.2004
203 West 233rd street, Bronx NY

Sketch prepared by:
Det. Brian F.Wilson
Shield # 1234 10/29/04 0930 hrs

FIGURE 7   Cross-projection sketch. All objects are drawn as if seen from above, but the walls are folded down and the items are drawn as if the room were a cardboard box with its sides flattened. Illustration courtesy of Brian Wilson, Medical Legal Art, © 2005, www.doereport.com. From Vernon Geberth, *Practical Homicide Investigation: Tactics, Procedures, and Forensic Techniques*, 4th ed. (Boca Raton, FL: CRC Press, 2006), 163.

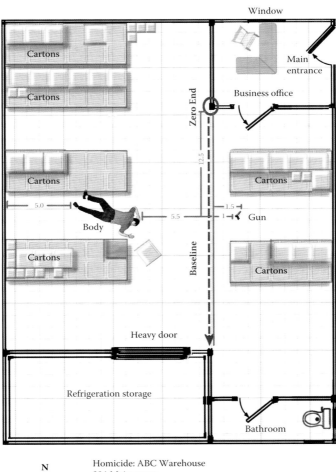

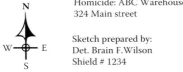

FIGURE 8 The baseline method of sketching can be used when there is a scene without a convenient straight line or boundaries such as a warehouse or large outdoor area. In this sketch, the cartons are moveable and the inside area is large. By drawing a baseline through the scene, you create a point of reference. Each end of the baseline should be identified, and there should be a starting point or zero ends. Illustration courtesy of Brian Wilson, Medical Legal Art, © 2005, www.doereport.com. From Vernon Geberth, *Practical Homicide Investigation: Tactics, Procedures, and Forensic Techniques*, 4th ed. (Boca Raton, FL: CRC Press, 2006), 164.

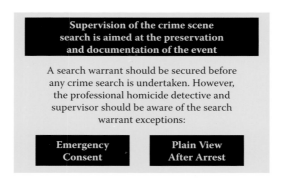

FIGURE 9 Search warrant exceptions.

Formulating the Search

The search for evidence begins with the isolation and protection of the scene. The searcher must ascertain that the scene is intact and then proceed to reconstruct the events that have transpired since his or her arrival.

Obviously, the best places for obtaining physical evidence are nearest to where the critical act occurred, such as in the immediate vicinity of the homicide victim. However, other areas related to the primary crime scene must not be overlooked, for example,

- ☐ The point of forced entry
- ☐ The route of escape
- ☐ The suspect (clothing, hands, body, hair, etc.)
- ☐ The location where the weapon is or may be located
- ☐ A vehicle that was used in the crime
- ☐ The suspect's residence
- ☐ The location where the assault leading to death took place
- ☐ The location from which the body was moved

In formulating the search plan, there may be some critical areas that you will want to cover immediately, or there may be some questions about what is or is not evidence. Don't be influenced by the original report, the police call, or any initial statements. Note this initial information, and then make your own determination based on the total information available.

Examination of the Outdoor Crime Scene

The investigator's actions at outdoor scenes are usually determined by the weather and the time of day. I have provided some practical procedures to follow. However, they are presented only as a guide. Each individual case will dictate how an investigator will retrieve evidence.

- ☐ Rope off the largest area possible, and secure the scene.
- ☐ Establish a path of entry and exit, usually the original path taken by the person who discovered the body. It should be examined for any possible trace evidence, then staked off or marked.
- ☐ All persons approaching the area should be cautioned to use this route and not deviate from the established path.
- ☐ The body and immediate surrounding area should be systematically examined before any weather or lighting conditions change. One of the recommended methods of crime scene search should be used (Figure 10 shows six search methods). Get additional people to the scene to implement this procedure.
- ☐ If the weather is obviously contributing to destroying, or about to destroy, trace evidence, collect the evidence as soon as possible even though some additional evidence may be missed, lost, or destroyed.

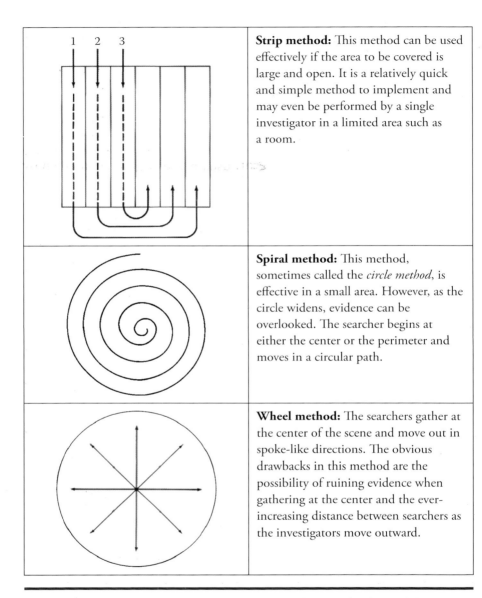

1　2　3	**Strip method:** This method can be used effectively if the area to be covered is large and open. It is a relatively quick and simple method to implement and may even be performed by a single investigator in a limited area such as a room.
	Spiral method: This method, sometimes called the *circle method*, is effective in a small area. However, as the circle widens, evidence can be overlooked. The searcher begins at either the center or the perimeter and moves in a circular path.
	Wheel method: The searchers gather at the center of the scene and move out in spoke-like directions. The obvious drawbacks in this method are the possibility of ruining evidence when gathering at the center and the ever-increasing distance between searchers as the investigators move outward.

FIGURE 10　Six search methods. These diagrams are reprinted with permission from Vernon Geberth, *Practical Homicide Investigation: Tactics, Procedures, and Forensic Techniques*, 4th ed. (Boca Raton, FL: CRC Press, 2006), 182–184.

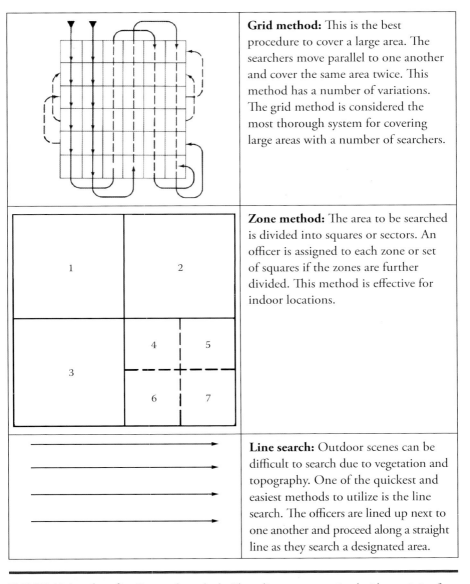

Grid method: This is the best procedure to cover a large area. The searchers move parallel to one another and cover the same area twice. This method has a number of variations. The grid method is considered the most thorough system for covering large areas with a number of searchers.

Zone method: The area to be searched is divided into squares or sectors. An officer is assigned to each zone or set of squares if the zones are further divided. This method is effective for indoor locations.

Line search: Outdoor scenes can be difficult to search due to vegetation and topography. One of the quickest and easiest methods to utilize is the line search. The officers are lined up next to one another and proceed along a straight line as they search a designated area.

FIGURE 10 (continued)   Six search methods. These diagrams are reprinted with permission from Vernon Geberth, *Practical Homicide Investigation: Tactics, Procedures, and Forensic Techniques*, 4th ed. (Boca Raton, FL: CRC Press, 2006), 182–184.

Investigative Questions

Ask yourself the following questions:

- ☐ Is the death caused by
    - ☐ Homicide?
    - ☐ Suicide?
    - ☐ Accident?
    - ☐ Natural causes?
- ☐ Do the facts, scene, statements, and physical evidence support this explanation?
- ☐ If the death is homicide:
    - ☐ What was the means or agency of death?
    - ☐ Is the homicide excusable or justifiable?
- ☐ Does it appear that any effort was made to purposely mislead the police? For example, could one of the following types of *staged crime scene* apply?
    - ☐ A simulated burglary
    - ☐ Arson
    - ☐ Murder made to look like suicide or accident
    - ☐ Suicide made to look like murder (insurance case?)
- ☐ Is there more than one possible cause of death?
- ☐ Are the witness statements consistent with the facts?
- ☐ Is the time element consistent with the condition of the scene?
- ☐ Are the bloodstains wet or dry?
- ☐ What is the condition of the body (rigor mortis, lividity, etc.)?
- ☐ Is there a weapon involved?
- ☐ Was more than one weapon used? What does this suggest?
    - ☐ Are the wounds consistent with the weapon suspected?
    - ☐ Is the weapon from the premises?
    - ☐ If the weapon was a firearm:
        1. Are any shell casings present?
        2. Are any bullet holes or spent rounds present on the ground, the walls, and/or the ceiling?
- ☐ Is a weapon under the body?
- ☐ Was the deceased armed?

During this self-cross-examination, do not make any final evaluation, since you are merely forming a hypothesis to assist you in planning the search. However, you should estimate as closely as possible the time and place of the homicide. In addition, you should have a general idea of how much evidence you plan to collect. During this stage, you will be depending on hard work, common sense, and keeping an open mind.

Examination of the Body at the Scene

The actual examination of the body should not begin until all photographs and sketches have been completed. In addition, a complete description of the body as well as any clothing must be obtained, including

- ☐ Sex
- ☐ Race
- ☐ Appearance
- ☐ Age
- ☐ Build
- ☐ Color of hair
- ☐ Evidence of injury and apparent cause of death
- ☐ Condition of the body (rigor mortis, lividity, etc.)
- ☐ Color of blood (wet or dry?)
- ☐ Position of body relative to objects of significance at the location

The investigator should then concentrate on recording a complete description of the clothing as follows:

- ☐ Position of clothes
- ☐ Condition of clothes (buttoned, unbuttoned, twisted sideways or pulled down, inside out, zippered or unzippered?)
- ☐ Damage to clothes (rips, tears, cuts, holes, etc.)
- ☐ Stains: blood, saliva, vomit, semen, phlegm, urine, or feces. Where are they? What are they? Is there any direction of flow?

After a complete description of the clothing and any significant position, condition, damage, or stains have been noted, the investigator begins a careful examination of the body starting with the head and working down to the legs and feet. This description will necessitate moving the body to look for any wounds or evidence of further injuries that were not visible in the original position.

The Head

- ☐ Are the eyes open or closed?
- ☐ Is the mouth open or closed?
- ☐ What is the position of the head in relation to the body?
- ☐ What is the color of the skin (lividity, etc.)?
- ☐ Is any blood present? (Describe.)
- ☐ Are there any visible wounds? (Describe.)
- ☐ Is there any foreign material on the head (soil, mud, etc.)?
- ☐ What is the condition of the deceased's hair (neat or messy)?
- ☐ Is any phlegm, saliva, vomit, blood, urine, semen, or feces present?

The Trunk

- ☐ The position of the trunk (twisted or bent over, on side or back, etc.)
- ☐ Any injuries? (Describe.)
- ☐ Presence of any stains (blood, semen, vomit, etc.)
- ☐ Presence of any hairs or fibers
- ☐ Presence of any foreign substances on the trunk (soil, mud, grease, tar, paint, etc.)

Arms and Legs

- ☐ Position of each arm and leg
- ☐ Presence of any injuries
- ☐ Presence of any stains
- ☐ Any foreign matter on the legs or arms?
- ☐ Are there any defensive wounds on the hands, arms, legs, or feet?

> *Remember*: **Note the presence or absence of any jewelry—rings, watches, etc., on the body, including any mark on the body indicating that such objects had been worn.**

Gunshot Wounds

Basically, when a firearm is discharged, the following dynamics occur:

1. Fire or flame is emitted from the barrel.
2. Smoke then follows this flame.
3. The bullet emerges from the barrel.
4. Additional smoke and grains of both burned and unburned gunpowder follow the bullet out of the barrel.
5. As this material exits the barrel, it spreads out like a funnel
6. As the distance from the barrel increases, the density of the pattern decreases.
7. The flame doesn't go very far, the smoke goes a little further, the powder grains travel different distances, and the bullet travels the greatest distance.
8. The bullet perforates the skin and bores through; the bullet entrance hole will be smaller than the actual projectile
9. There will be a blackening effect around the wound's edges caused by the discharge of lubricants, smoke particles, and grime from the barrel of the weapon.

Figure 12 differentiates firearm injuries between distance and contact wounds, and Figure 13 shows the difference between close shots at shorter and farther distances. See Figure 14 for an example of a close- to intermediate-range wound, Figure 15 for a self-inflicted shotgun wound, Figure 16 for a wound dynamics diagram, and Figure 17 for a diagram of a contact wound.

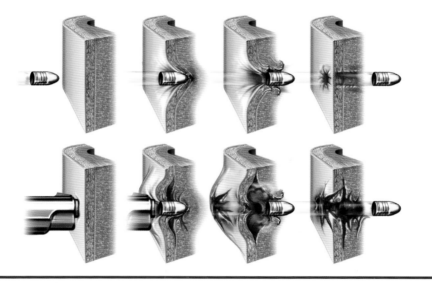

FIGURE 12 Firearms injuries: differences between distance and contact wounds. Illustration courtesy of Brian Wilson, Medical Legal Art, © 2005, www.doereport.com.

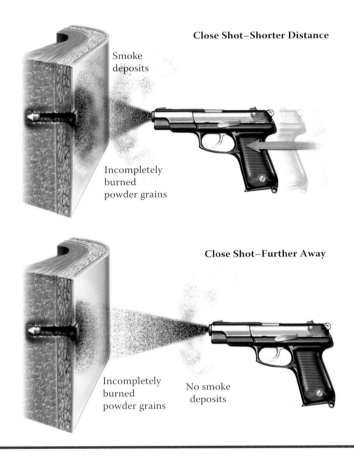

FIGURE 13   Close-range firearms injuries. Illustrations courtesy of Brian Wilson, Medical Legal Art, © 2005, www.doereport.com. Permission from Vernon Geberth, *Practical Homicide Investigation: Tactics, Procedures, and Forensic Techniques*, 4th ed. (Boca Raton, FL: CRC Press, 2006), 316.

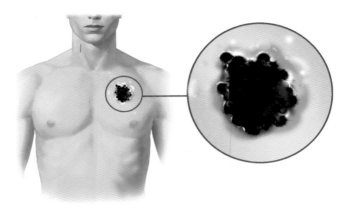

FIGURE 14   Close- to intermediate-range shotgun wounds. The muzzle of the weapon is held away from the body but close enough to cause a circular or oval shape around the entrance wound. Illustration courtesy of Brian Wilson, Medical Legal Art, © 2012, www.doereport.com.

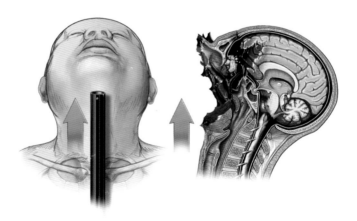

FIGURE 15   Self-inflicted shotgun wound under the chin. These types of wounds cause massive tissue destruction, usually obliterating the victim's face and head. Illustration courtesy of Brian Wilson, Medical Legal Art, © 2012, www.doereport.com.

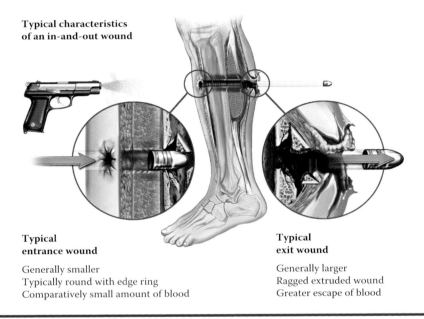

Typical characteristics
of an in-and-out wound

**Typical
entrance wound**

Generally smaller
Typically round with edge ring
Comparatively small amount of blood

**Typical
exit wound**

Generally larger
Ragged extruded wound
Greater escape of blood

FIGURE 16 **Diagram of wound dynamics:** Typical characteristics of in-and-out wounds, which follow a general configuration. There are many exceptions. Illustration courtesy of Brian Wilson, Medical Legal Art, © 2005, www.doereport.com. Permission from Vernon Geberth, *Practical Homicide Investigation: Tactics, Procedures, and Forensic Techniques*, 4th ed. (Boca Raton, FL: CRC Press, 2006), 319.

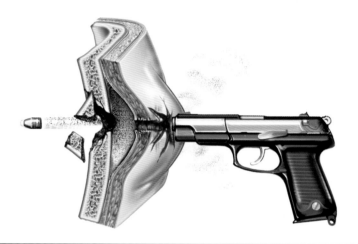

FIGURE 17   Diagram representation of a contact wound. The weapon is pressed against the head or body in an area overlying bone surfaces. Subsequently, the gases from the explosion expand between the skin and the underlying bone surfaces producing a bursting effect with a ragged entrance wound. Illustration courtesy of Brian Wilson, Medical Legal Art, © 2005, www.doereport.com. Permission from Vernon Geberth, Practical Homicide Investigation: Tactics, Procedures, and Forensic Techniques, 4th ed. (Boca Raton, FL: CRC Press, 2006), 327.

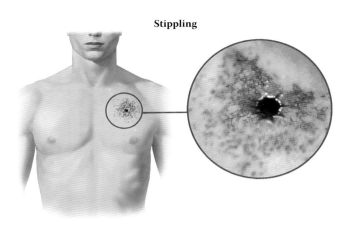

Stippling

FIGURE 18 Tattooing or stippling. The bullet entrance is surrounded by pinpoint hemorrhages due to the discharge of burned powder and fragments, which have been driven into the skin. This is the result of a close-range shot. Illustration courtesy of Brian Wilson, Medical Legal Art, © 2012, www.doereport.com.

Intermediate-Range Wounds

In these wounds, the muzzle of the weapon is held away from the body, but near enough for powder particles to be projected onto the skin. So in addition to tattooing (see Figure 18), soot may also be deposited.

Cutting Wounds

An incision or cut-type wound is caused by a sharp instrument or weapon and is generally longer than it is deep. The cut or incised wound is deepest where the weapon was first applied to the skin. If the cutting is done parallel to the lines of cleavage, the edges of the wound will remain together. If the cutting is across the lines of cleavage, the wound will be gaping or open. See Figures 19–22 for examples of cutting wounds.

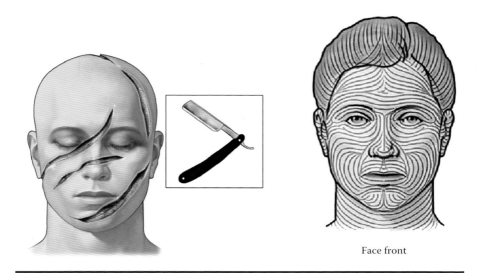

Face front

FIGURE 19   Incised wounds—straight razor. The illustration at left depicts homicidal-type injuries inflicted with a straight razor. Note that the wounds are longer than deep and will bleed profusely. These types of injuries cut across the lines of cleavage (see illustration at right) and usually result in permanent scarring for victims who survive the assault. Illustrations courtesy of Brian Wilson, Medical Legal Art, © 2012, www.doereport.com.

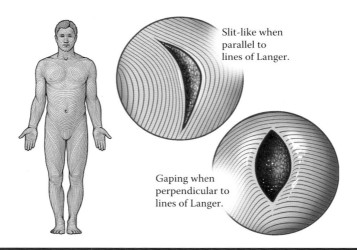

Slit-like when parallel to lines of Langer.

Gaping when perpendicular to lines of Langer.

FIGURE 20   Lines of cleavage or Langer's lines. The cutting injury will appear slit-like when cut parallel to the lines of Langer. The cutting injury will have a gaping effect when perpendicular to the lines of Langer. Illustration courtesy of Brian Wilson, Medical Legal Art, © 2012, www.doereport.com.

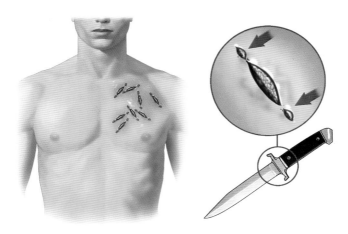

FIGURE 21   Multiple stabbing wounds. In multiple deep, penetrating, stabbing wounds, there may be the presence of hilt marks from the weapon employed by the assailant, which form a pattern injury on the skin. Illustration courtesy of Brian Wilson, Medical Legal Art, © 2012, www.doereport.com.

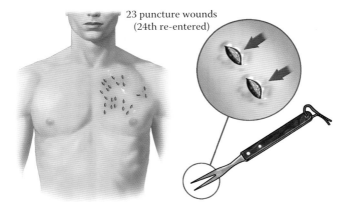

FIGURE 22   Multiple stabbing wounds with a two-prong barbeque fork. Illustration courtesy of Brian Wilson, Medical Legal Art, © 2012, www.doereport.com.

Blunt Force Injuries

Blunt force injuries are usually evident by outward signs such as lacerations and bruising. However, lack of external injuries does not mean that blunt force was not applied. In many cases, internal damage to organs occurs without any external signs of violence. The abdominal organs are vulnerable to a variety of injuries because of the lax and compressible abdominal walls.

In homicide and death investigation, we look for impact injuries to the head which were caused by an object striking the head or the head striking an object. See Figures 23 and 24 for examples of blunt force injuries.

FIGURE 23   Examples of blunt force injuries: injuries caused by (top) a hammer, and (bottom) a rock. Illustrations courtesy of Brian Wilson, Medical Legal Art, © 2012, www.doereport.com.

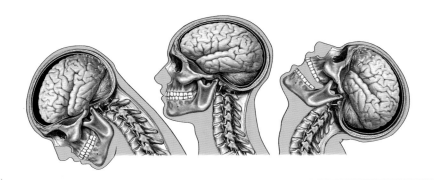

FIGURE 24 **The types of physiological derangements which occur in a contrecoup injury.** The injury contralateral to the coup injury causes internal bleeding of the brain. Illustrations courtesy of Brian Wilson, Medical Legal Art, © 2012, www.doereport.com.

Asphyxial Deaths

Deaths by asphyxia can occur through any number of circumstances. The most common are strangulation, suffocation, mechanical or positional asphyxia, drowning, smothering, choking, hanging, confined spaces, and traumatic asphyxia. Any death in which air is cut off from the victim is considered to be asphyxial in nature. (See Figures 25 and 26.)

Figures 27 through 34 illustrate different types of asphyxiation as well as related injuries that also occur in cases of child abuse and/or sexual assault.

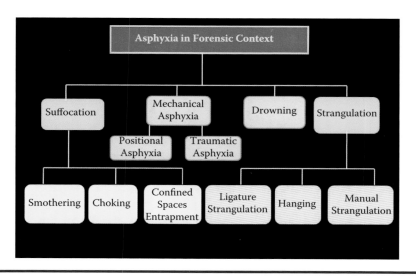

FIGURE 25   Asphyxia in a forensic context.

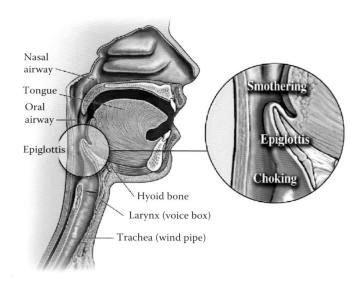

FIGURE 26   Anatomy of the upper airway. Illustration courtesy of Brian Wilson, Medical Legal Art, © 2012, www.doereport.com.

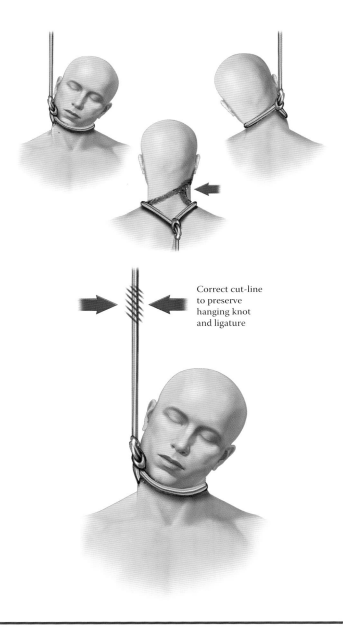

Correct cut-line
to preserve
hanging knot
and ligature

FIGURE 27 **Top: Hanging**—strangulation by means of a rope, cord, or similar ligature tightened by the weight of the body. **Bottom: Correct cut line to preserve a hanging knot and ligature.** Illustrations courtesy of Brian Wilson, Medical Legal Art, © 2012, www.doereport.com.

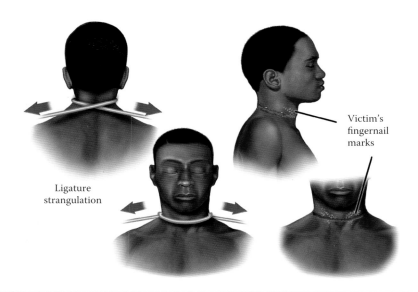

FIGURE 28   **Ligature or mechanical strangulation.** This type of strangulation involves pressure on the neck caused by a constricting band around it, usually a rope, wire, or piece of clothing. This will usually leave a groove mark and sometimes the marks of the victim's fingernails as they attempt to loosen the ligature from their neck. Illustration courtesy of Brian Wilson, Medical Legal Art, © 2013, www.doereport.com.

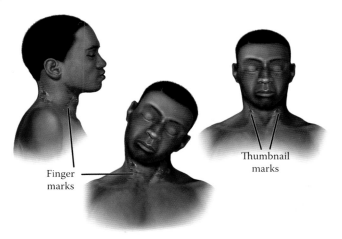

FIGURE 29   **Manual strangulation.** There may be fractures of the hyoid bone or thyroid cartilage accompanied by hemorrhage. There also may be thumb or fingernail impressions on the skin of the victim's neck. Illustration courtesy of Brian Wilson, Medical Legal Art, © 2012, www.doereport.com.

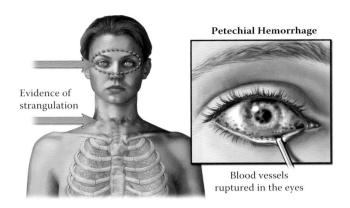

FIGURE 30 **Petechial hemorrhage** consists of minute (pin-like) hemorrhages that occur at points beneath the skin. They are usually observed in the conjunctivae, the mucous membrane lining the inner surface of the eyelids and anterior part of the sclera. Illustration courtesy of Brian Wilson, Medical Legal Art, © 2008, www.doereport.com.

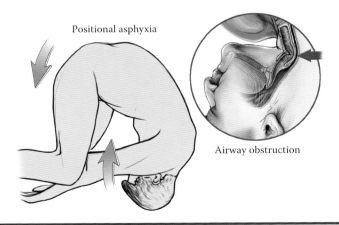

FIGURE 31 **Positional asphyxia** can occur when a person's position prevents him or her from breathing adequately. This can occur through carelessness or as a consequence of an accident. An example would be someone who became intoxicated and fell into a breathing-restricted position. Illustration courtesy of Brian Wilson, Medical Legal Art, © 2012, www.doereport.com.

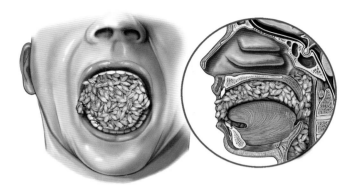

FIGURE 32 Choking diagram. Asphyxia by choking is caused by obstruction of the air passages below the epiglottis. Illustration courtesy of Brian Wilson, Medical Legal Art, © 2012, www.doereport. com.

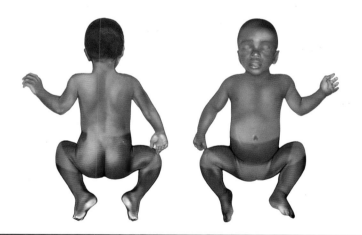

FIGURE 33 Usual distribution of scalding burns on children, with the sparing of knees, popliteal fossae, and inguinal regions. When the child is lowered into the high-temperature water, it contacts the feet first. This causes an involuntary withdrawal of the feet such that there is a flexion at the knees and hips. The child is thus immersed in a squatting position. Illustration courtesy of Brian Wilson, Medical Legal Art, © 2012, www.doereport.com.

FIGURE 34   **Torn frenulum.** The presence of a torn frenulum inside the mouth is indicative of a physical assault usually caused by a punch to the victim's mouth; it is commonly seen in sexual assault and child abuse cases. Illustration courtesy of Brian Wilson, Medical Legal Art, © 2012, www.doereport.com.

Recommendations and Guidelines for Proper Death Notifications to Surviving Family Members

The following recommendations and guidelines are based upon my personal experience in making death notifications as well as information from the *Revised Homicide and Sudden Death Survivor Guidelines*, established by the attorney general of the State of New Jersey, available at www.state.nj.us/lps/dcj/agguide/homicide.htm; the National Organization for Victim Assistance (NOVA), *Community Crisis Response Team Training Manual*, 2nd ed. (Washington, DC: U.S. Department of Justice, 1994); and research developed by the National Victim Center.

☐ Notification should be made in person by the assigned detective as soon as possible after identity has been established. *Under no circumstances should the media be advised of an identification prior to next of kin.*

- ☐ Try to assure that the appropriate closest adult relative receives notification first.
- ☐ Get as much information about the person(s) to be notified as possible. Medical information (e.g., a heart condition) about the person to be notified is particularly important, if available.
- ☐ Identify yourself as the assigned detective, and present your credentials. Request permission to enter the home.
- ☐ Encourage survivors to sit, and sit down with them when you talk to them.
- ☐ Make sure there are no dangerous objects nearby. This includes scissors, knives, heavy objects, etc.
- ☐ Make the actual notification of death simply and directly: "I have some bad news for you. Your son is dead." Tell the surviving family that you are sorry for their loss, and express to them your condolences in a professional and empathic manner.
- ☐ Answer all questions tactfully and honestly *without jeopardizing the criminal investigation.*
- ☐ Be prepared to explain what happened, when it happened, where it happened, and how it happened. Be prepared to present confirming evidence and the source of positive identification in a clear and convincing fashion in the face of denial.
- ☐ After the survivors have recovered from the initial shock, explain that you need to ask certain informational questions about the deceased in order to initiate the investigation and that you will try to keep these questions as brief as possible.
- ☐ Explain that it will be necessary for a family member to identify the deceased. Allow the family to choose who will make the identification.
- ☐ Transport this family member, or arrange for his or her transportation, to and from the hospital or morgue.
- ☐ Inform the survivors that a medicolegal autopsy is required to establish the exact cause of death.
- ☐ Focus on the immediate needs of the survivors. Offer to assist them in notifying and contacting others, e.g., "Is there someone I can call to see if they could come over now?"

- ☐ Make sure that the survivors are not left alone. Have an officer or crisis worker remain pending the arrival of some designated friend or relative.
- ☐ Explain that you will be available for any questions and provide your business card and office telephone number.
- ☐ Offer information on crime victims services by providing the telephone number(s).
- ☐ If the survivor is at her or his place of employment, the notifying officers should proceed there, contact the survivor's supervisor, and request to speak privately with the survivor so proper notification can be made.
- ☐ In some instances, the survivors of sudden and violent death are not immediately available. In these circumstances, the officers should make inquiries of neighbors to ascertain when the family is expected home. Explain that there has been a medical emergency involving the deceased and request the neighbor to contact them if the survivors return home.
- ☐ The officers should request that the neighbor not provide the next of kin with any information regarding the medical emergency until the officers contact them.
- ☐ If surviving family members do not reside within the jurisdiction responsible for investigating the death, or within a reasonable distance of that jurisdiction, the detective should contact the appropriate law enforcement agency which covers the residence of the family.
- ☐ That agency should be requested to make an in-person notification to the surviving family and provide the family with the investigating officer's name, agency, and telephone number.

Sex-Related Homicide Investigation

Investigative Considerations

Sex-related homicides include rape murders, serial murders, killings which involve both anal and oral sodomy and other acts of sexual perversion, as well as sexually oriented interpersonal violence cases.

A homicide is classified as sex-related when there is evidence of sexual activity observed in the crime scene or upon the body of the victim. This includes

- ☐ The type of, or lack of, attire on the victim
- ☐ Evidence of seminal fluid on, near, or in the body
- ☐ Evidence of sexual injury and/or sexual mutilation
- ☐ Sexualized positioning of the body
- ☐ Evidence of substitute sexual activity (e.g., fantasy, ritualism, symbolism, and/or masturbation)
- ☐ Multiple stabbing or cuttings to the body; this includes slicing wounds across the abdomen of the victim, throat slashing, and overkill-type injuries, which are considered highly suggestive of a sexual motivation.

For further information, refer to Chapters 14 and 15 in *Practical Homicide Investigation: Tactics, Procedures, and Forensic Techniques*, 4th ed. (Boca Raton, FL: CRC Press, 2006); or *Sex-Related Homicide and Death Investigation: Practical and Clinical Perspectives* (Boca Raton, FL: CRC Press, 2010).

The Crime Scene Investigation

The search of the homicide crime scene is the most important phase of the investigation conducted at the scene. It begins with a twofold purpose:

1. The complete documentation of events. Photographs (both black and white and color), videotape, as well as crime scene sketches should be accomplished prior to any other police procedures at the scene.
2. A careful and complete search should be conducted for any forensic materials and other evidence which might provide a clue to the identity of the killer.

Sex-Related Crime Scene Checklist

- ☐ Physical evidence in the form of seminal fluid must be collected as soon as possible before it is lost or destroyed. Samples can be allowed to air dry naturally, or you can use a hair dryer on low speed. Wet samples can be drawn into an eyedropper and should be placed in a sterile test tube. *Submit for DNA testing.*

☐ Dry stains will have a stiff "starchy" texture. If on clothing, submit entire article, being careful not to break or contaminate the stained area. *Submit for DNA testing.*

☐ Blood (wet) should be collected using an eyedropper and transferred to a sterile container. The blood can be put into a test tube with EDTA, an anticoagulant, and refrigerated. Small amounts can be collected using a 100% cotton swab, #8 cotton thread, or gauze pad. Allow swab or material to air dry, and place in a sterile container. *Consider DNA testing techniques.*

☐ Bloodstain, spittle, and hair (including pubic combings) should be obtained at the scene, properly packaged, and forwarded to the lab. *Consider DNA testing techniques.*

☐ Trace evidence found on the victim and/or upon victim's clothing should be collected. Search for hair, fibers, and other microscopic evidence. Use forceps, a vacuum cleaner fitted with an inline canister attachment in the hose, or tape. Tape and forceps are the best method to avoid contamination of the samples.

☐ Bruises and marks on the victim, including the presence of sadistic injuries, should be noted and documented in the investigative notes.

☐ Urine or feces may be left at the scene by the assailant. This evidence should be recorded and collected. Urine can be removed by eyedropper or gauze. Place in a sterile test tube or other container. If on clothing, submit entire article. *DNA testing can be performed on urine.*

☐ Fingernail scrapings should be obtained for an analysis of any blood, skin, or hair from the perpetrator. *Consider DNA testing techniques.*

☐ Confer with the medical examiner and assure that specimens are taken from the body (e.g., hair from various areas of the body). In addition, vaginal washings, as well as anal, nasal, and oral swabs, should be requested for serological evaluation and examination. *Consider DNA testing techniques.*

☐ Examine the scene for evidence of a struggle. The presence of torn clothing, missing buttons, ripped textiles, marks on the ground or floor, and blood splatters must all be photographed, documented, and collected as evidence.

- [ ] Homicides involving mutilation may yield clues such as style of attack, the type of weapon used, the amount and location of mutilation, and the position of the body. These items should be recorded. (See Chapter 21, "Investigative Assessment Criminal Personality Profiling," in *Practical Homicide Investigation: Tactics, Procedures, and Forensic Techniques*, 4th ed. (Boca Raton, FL: CRC Press, 2006) for further information.)
- [ ] If a suspect has been taken into custody, his or her clothing should be taken, and an examination conducted for any physical evidence. Examine for hairs and fibers.
- [ ] Each piece of evidence should be packaged in a separate container in order to prevent cross-contamination.
- [ ] The suspect's body should be examined for any fingernail scratches, bite marks, or other indications of a violent struggle.
- [ ] Hair and blood samples should be obtained from the suspect's body. (Assure that any such samples from the suspect are obtained legally.)
- [ ] The suspect's body should be examined for the presence of bite-mark evidence. For any bite marks found, collect and record:
  - [ ] Saliva washing of the bite-mark area for blood grouping. Use 100% sterile cotton swabs dampened in distilled water. *Important*: Obtain a control sample from another area of the body.
  - [ ] Photograph the bite mark. Obtain black-and-white and color photos. Use a rule of measure, and obtain an anatomical landmark.
  - [ ] Cast the bite mark (if possible). Use dental materials.

See the Appendix for further information on collecting bite-mark evidence.

Medicolegal Considerations

Examination of the Crime Scene

In many jurisdictions, a medical investigator, medical examiner, or coroner will respond to the crime scene to ascertain the essential facts concerning the circumstances of death and make a preliminary examination of the body.

The medical examiner or coroner takes charge of the body, any clothing on the body, and any article on or near the body that may assist the pathologist in determining the cause and manner of death.

If the medical examiner or coroner does not respond, the homicide detective who conducted the preliminary police investigation and was present at the crime scene should attend the autopsy and provide the medical examiner or coroner with the following information.

Descriptive Information

- [ ] Description of the circumstances of death
- [ ] Description of the scene of death (Complete notes taken at the scene include a description of the deceased, color of any blood, injuries and wounds observed, etc.)
- [ ] Condition of the body when first discovered (rigor mortis, lividity, temperature, putrefaction, decomposition, maggots or other insect activity, etc.)
- [ ] Statements taken from witnesses and/or suspects
- [ ] Police photographs taken at the scene (Digital photos can be taken in addition to the usual police photos since they are ready for viewing immediately and can be available at autopsy.)
- [ ] Diagrams and sketches of the crime scene
- [ ] Any weapons or articles found at the scene which relate to the death (knives, guns, other weapons, notes, paper, drugs, etc.).
- [ ] Any questions formulated during the initial phase of the investigation; these may be evaluated in light of the medical evidence found by the pathologist.

Anatomical Figures

Figures 35 through 42 present anatomical guides that are useful for homicide investigations.

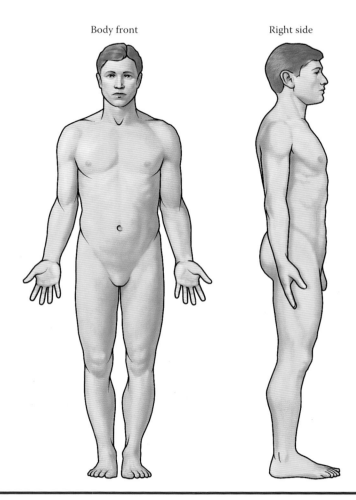

FIGURE 35   Anatomical position—wound chart. Illustration courtesy of Brian Wilson, Medical Legal Art, © 2005, www.doereport.com. Used with permission from Vernon Geberth, *Practical Homicide Investigation: Tactics, Procedures, and Forensic Techniques*, 4th ed. (Boca Raton, FL: CRC Press, 2006), 197.

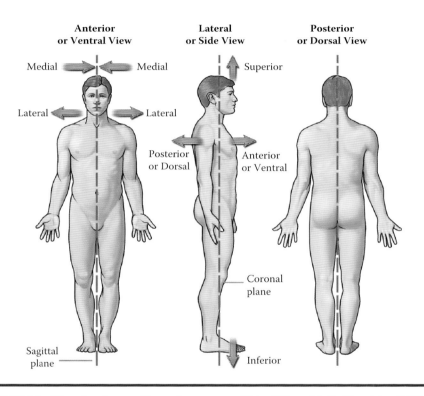

FIGURE 36 **Directional terms.** Illustration courtesy of Brian Wilson, Medical Legal Art, © 2005, www.doereport.com. Used with permission from Vernon Geberth, *Practical Homicide Investigation: Tactics, Procedures, and Forensic Techniques*, 4th ed. (Boca Raton, FL: CRC Press, 2006), 666.

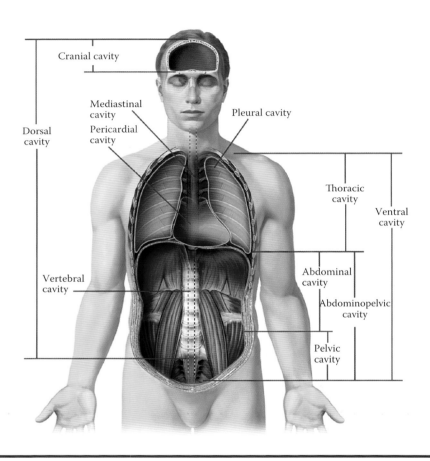

FIGURE 37   Body cavities. Illustration courtesy of Brian Wilson, Medical Legal Art, © 2005, www.doereport.com. Used with permission from Vernon Geberth, *Practical Homicide Investigation: Tactics, Procedures, and Forensic Techniques*, 4th ed. (Boca Raton, FL: CRC Press, 2006), 667.

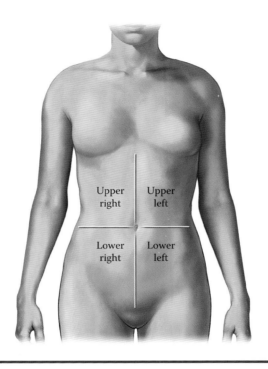

FIGURE 38   Quadrants. Illustration courtesy of Brian Wilson, Medical Legal Art, © 2005, www. doereport.com. Used with permission from Vernon Geberth, *Practical Homicide Investigation: Tactics, Procedures, and Forensic Techniques*, 4th ed. (Boca Raton, FL: CRC Press, 2006), 668.

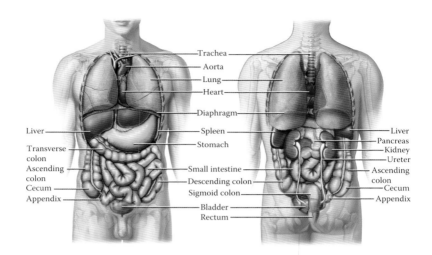

FIGURE 39   Anterior and posterior views of the thoracic and abdominal cavities. Illustration courtesy of Brian Wilson, Medical Legal Art, © 2005, www.doereport.com. Used with permission from Vernon Geberth, *Practical Homicide Investigation: Tactics, Procedures, and Forensic Techniques*, 4th ed. (Boca Raton, FL: CRC Press, 2006), 669.

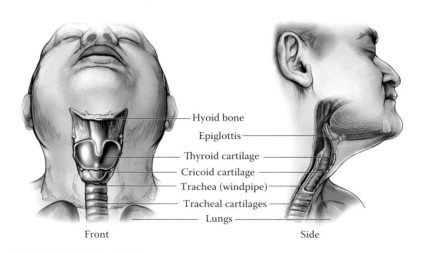

FIGURE 40   Anatomy of the larynx. Illustration courtesy of Brian Wilson, Medical Legal Art, © 2005, www.doereport.com. Used with permission from Vernon Geberth, *Practical Homicide Investigation: Tactics, Procedures, and Forensic Techniques*, 4th ed. (Boca Raton, FL: CRC Press, 2006), 668.

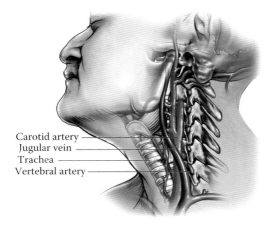

Carotid artery
Jugular vein
Trachea
Vertebral artery

FIGURE 41   Arteries and veins in the neck. Illustration courtesy of Brian Wilson, Medical Legal Art, © 2005, www.doereport.com. Used with permission from Vernon Geberth, *Practical Homicide Investigation: Tactics, Procedures, and Forensic Techniques*, 4th ed. (Boca Raton, FL: CRC Press, 2006), 668.

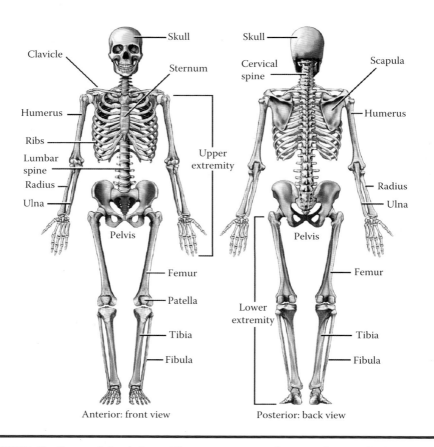

FIGURE 42   **Bones of the skeleton.** Illustration courtesy of Brian Wilson, Medical Legal Art, © 2005, www.doereport.com. Used with permission from Vernon Geberth, *Practical Homicide Investigation: Tactics, Procedures, and Forensic Techniques,* 4th ed. (Boca Raton, FL: CRC Press, 2006), 672.

Supervisor's Homicide Checklist

*Supervising the Preliminary Investigation
at the Scene: The Checklist*

- [ ] *Initial receipt of information*: It is imperative that the supervisor, upon being notified that detectives are requested to respond to a possible homicide, record the following information:
  - [ ] Date and time received
  - [ ] How initial report was received
  - [ ] Name of person making report (this includes police officers)
  - [ ] Complete details

  At this point, the homicide supervisor either responds directly with investigators in their unit, or responds with his or her own unit. I recommend that the supervisor take his or her own unit to the scene.

- [ ] *Assign a member to maintain communications within the command*: This member's responsibility will be to make follow-up notifications, record checks and requests for special services, as well as take requests from the command post at the crime scene. This assignment becomes critical in major-case investigations when overhead commands attempt to assess the investigation.
- [ ] Duties upon arrival at the scene:
  - [ ] Record the exact time of arrival
  - [ ] Record the exact address
  - [ ] Record police units present
  - [ ] Confer with detectives at the scene. Ascertain that there is an investigator assigned to the case. If an investigator has not been officially assigned as *case officer*, assign one immediately.
- [ ] Confer with uniformed supervisor, and establish cooperation.
  - [ ] Confer with first officer, and obtain a quick briefing.
  - [ ] Make a visual inspection of the crime scene and victim. Have the first officer or detective escort you in order to get a feel for the case and establish perimeters.

☐ Solicit any opinions and/or theories from police personnel at the scene. Evaluate these with your own observations.

☐ Determine any investigative needs, and make assignments as necessary.

☐ Establish your authority by providing any personnel and/or equipment.

☐ Implement an assignment sheet. Record assignments, know who is performing what assignment to assist in the coordination effort.

☐ The supervisor's notebook becomes a log detailing exactly who has what assignment. This enables the supervisor to properly assign team members and record exactly what has transpired at the crime scene. As members report back, the supervisor jots down a brief paragraph detailing their activities. Later, this notebook can be utilized to conduct the investigative critique and designate responsibility for the subsequent written reports.

☐ *Initiate an investigative canvass*: The investigative canvass is simply a door-to-door inquiry or roadblock operation in order to obtain information and/or locate witnesses.

Remember: **The supervisor should assign a sufficient number of officers to effectively cover the area to be canvassed. I recommend assigning a supervisor to coordinate the canvass and instructing members to use canvass questionnaires and canvass control sheets for effective follow-up surveys.**

☐ *Victim removed to hospital*: If the victim has been removed to a hospital, assign either a patrol unit or detective to respond to the hospital to assure proper evidence collection procedures (re: clothing, ID papers, etc.) are undertaken. In addition, there may be an opportunity to obtain a dying declaration.

☐ *Transmittal of alarms*: Ascertain what alarms have been transmitted. Review alarms for appropriate information and consider updating them based upon information developed at the scene.

☐ *Dissemination of information*: Provide for the dissemination of information to all units and personnel involved in the investigation.

Keep the command post and investigators informed of all relative and current information as it becomes available.

☐ *Handling curious onlookers*: Utilize patrol officers to maintain lines, and instruct detectives to use courtesy and tact in dealing with people at the scene.

> ☐ Assign members in street clothes to "work the crowd" to obtain any overhears, direct bilingual officers to mingle with bystanders, etc. (depending upon circumstances).
>
> ☐ Direct that photos be taken of the crowd.

☐ *Interview ambulance personnel*: Direct that ambulance or emergency medical services (EMS) personnel be interviewed if they arrived before relative to their activities at the scene as well as any persons they may have seen or things they may have overheard.

Directing Specific Investigative Duties

The Suspect in Custody

☐ Establish probable cause for arrest.

☐ Determine the scope of the preliminary investigation.

☐ Ascertain the location of any evidence.

☐ Advise detectives to instruct patrol officers to document their observations (re: any overhears or statements, and any information provided by informants and/or witnesses).

☐ Interview and interrogate suspect in custody.

> ☐ Direct investigators to document their Miranda warnings.
>
> ☐ If the suspect is cooperative, have detectives take a preliminary statement at the scene, which can be used to assist in the recovery of any evidence, etc.

☐ Formal interrogation: This is best undertaken at the station house.

☐ Direct that no one interfere with an investigator who is in the process of taking a statement from a suspect.

> **Remember**: **The cardinal rule of interrogation is "Never intrude on an interview of a suspect." This includes supervisors as well.**

Examination of a Suspect for Evidence

☐ Advise investigators to document by both photography and sketches any scratches, bruises, injuries, etc., observed on the suspect.

☐ Advise transporting officers to be aware of evidential considerations. (Do not allow suspect to wash.)

☐ Dying declarations: Anytime you have a seriously injured victim, a consideration should be made to obtain a dying declaration.

☐ Direct investigators to respond to the hospital, obtain a witness if possible, and attempt to obtain a statement from the injured victim.

There are no set guidelines for the exact sequence of questions. Basically, you want to first establish that the victim is competent and lucid and believes that he or she is about to die.

Evaluation of a Suspect's Demeanor and/or Mental Capacity

☐ Direct detectives to document the suspect's demeanor and/or mental capacity from the time of arrest to arraignment. This procedure is necessary to prepare against a possible *diminished capacity defense.*

Supervising a Homicide Crime Scene Search

Supervision of the investigation conducted at the scene is a *separate* and *distinct* function. Ideally, there should be a crime scene investigator or evidence technician assigned to conduct the search. I recommend that departments select and train a sufficient number of investigators for this extremely important function.

Remember: **People have come to expect that evidence of a crime will be found and retrieved by police investigators at the scenes of crimes. The "CSI effect," in which jurors assume that evidence is *always* found at crime scenes because they have seen this occur on CSI and other television productions, has created this perception. *This may not be true in all instances.***

Therefore, consider and document the environment, conditions, and/or crime scene contamination. Often agencies do not put enough emphasis on this phase of the investigation, opting instead for something less time-consuming (e.g., a confession).

Make sure you do a proper search.

The purpose of the crime scene search is to obtain evidence. The function of the supervisor is to document and preserve the event. Practically speaking, if there is any possibility that any evidence you are about to seize for use in a homicide prosecution requires a search warrant, it is your job as the *supervisor* to assure that this warrant is obtained. Supervisors should also be aware of warrant exceptions: emergency, items in plain view, items seized with their owner's consent, and searches of persons after arrest.

Practically speaking, any method of search can be used, depending on the size, location, and complexity of the scene, as long as the search is *systematic* and *complete*.

The scope of the search is usually determined by a hypothesis arrived at by the detective supervisor and investigators based upon their initial observations of the scene. This hypothesis (sometimes informally called a *theory*), which is provisional, is based upon simple assumptions of how and why the homicide occurred.

Remember: Anything and everything can be evidence.

Crime Scene Considerations

The primary responsibility is the isolation and protection of the crime scene. The objective is to establish the *corpus delicti* and the identity of the criminal.

Preliminary Steps

- ☐ Upon arrival, ascertain boundaries. Do not move blindly into an area (confer before moving).
- ☐ Decide how to approach the crime scene. Determine paths of entry and exit (confer with first officer, etc.).

☐ Make the initial survey (escorted by first officer). Use this opportunity to develop a mental image.

☐ Ascertain whether any fragile evidence is present (assure collection).

☐ Prior to any crime scene search, direct that crime scene photographs and sketches be made.

☐ Make a supervisory hypothesis, as follows: Ask yourself what happened. Keep an open mind; don't be influenced by the original report, the police call, or initial statements. Note all the information. Make your own determination based upon the total information available. Was the death caused by homicide, suicide, an accident, or natural causes? The answer to this question is based upon the facts, crime scene, statements, and physical evidence supporting this explanation.

Remember: **Things are not always as they appear to be. Don't be afraid to change your mind. Any hypothesis is only provisional at best.**

Examination of the Body at the Scene

☐ Direct that all photographs and sketches be completed before examining the body.

☐ Direct that a complete description of the body as well as clothing be obtained.

☐ Portions of the body which were not accessible prior to the photos can now be examined and photographed.

☐ Direct a complete examination of the body, note wounds, and direct that this information be recorded.

Release of the Body

☐ *Release of the body*: This decision is critical. Once the body is released from the scene, *no additional procedures can be undertaken* (e.g., photographs).

   ☐ Direct that the body be wrapped in a clean white sheet before being placed in a body bag.

Examining an Outdoor Crime Scene

When examining an outdoor crime scene, direct the following:

- ☐ Rope off the largest area.
- ☐ Establish a path of entry and exit.
- ☐ Conduct examination as soon as possible (before losing daylight or experiencing weather changes).
- ☐ Direct that surrounding area be searched.
- ☐ If weather changes suddenly, order that evidence be collected immediately.

Examining an Outdoor Scene at Night

Under ordinary circumstances, an outdoor scene should not be searched during nighttime hours—this is common sense. Direct the following:

- ☐ Safeguard and secure the area.
- ☐ Direct that photographs be taken before body is moved.
- ☐ Safeguard body against additional damage in transport.

> *Remember*: Searches should be postponed until daylight because it is utterly impossible to discover or detect minute traces of evidence under nighttime conditions.
>
> Weather changes the rule. *Under no circumstances should the crime scene and/or body be left unguarded and unprotected until daylight hours.* Assign sufficient coverage for the purposes of maintaining the "chain of custody."

Release of the Crime Scene

- ☐ *Release of the crime scene*: This decision is critical. Practically speaking, the authorities should hold on to the scene as long as possible. There may be a need for additional photos, information may reveal the need to collect additional materials, an additional search may be necessary, and so on.

Before releasing the crime scene, consider: A good defense attorney will visit the crime scene to judge the extent of the police investigation. He or she will be alert to areas that were or were not processed.

☐ Recommended procedure:
  ☐ Direct that all materials used to process the scene be placed in a receptacle that can be taken from the scene when the police leave.
  ☐ Direct members to make sure that all police equipment has been secured and removed from the premises before release.

Investigation of Police-Related Shootings

Officer-Involved Shootings (OISs) and Use of Deadly Force Incidents

Police-related shooting incidents (OISs and incidents involving the use of deadly force) involve the discharge of a firearm by a sworn officer in the performance of duty resulting in injury or death. The necessary and appropriate use of this authority is an awesome responsibility. The decision to use deadly force is based on the circumstances as presented at the time of the incident. The final determination of justification, however, is based on law.

The official police investigation usually concentrates on the issue of whether the officer acted within the agency's guidelines. The determination is based upon the law as it relates to the "justifiable use of force," ethics, good judgment, and departmental policies established within the agency. The author acknowledges that there may be variances in the law, and case management and/or investigative techniques are usually determined on a jurisdiction-by-jurisdiction basis.

In situations where a death has occurred in connection with a police-related shooting incident, I personally recommend that a homicide investigation take precedence over any type of internal investigation inquiry. An internal investigation can always be conducted after the homicide probe.

The Protocol

In this section, I have incorporated the suggestions and protocols recommended by David E. Hatch of the Las Vegas Metropolitan Police

Department in his *Officer-Involved Shootings and the Use of Force: Practical Investigative Techniques* (Boca Raton, FL: CRC Press, 2002).

Introduction

The purpose of the protocol is to focus primarily on the responsibilities for investigating OISs and use of deadly force incidents. The seriousness of an OIS cannot be overstated; nothing can impact an agency's reputation and the involved employee's career more than a use of deadly force incident.

Assigning Investigative Responsibility

Investigative responsibility depends on the resources and expertise available to an agency. Responsibility for conducting the investigation is of paramount importance.

Internal Affairs Units should *NOT* be considered for investigative responsibility. A use of deadly force incident is not, by definition, an internal investigation; it is a very public event and subject to public scrutiny.

Investigation of OISs and Use of Deadly Force Incidents

Supervisory Responsibilities—Checklist

☐ Upon being made aware of an OIS, the investigative supervisor should contact on-scene supervisory personnel or senior officer at the scene to be briefed (via cellular phone or land line) as to the nature of this incident, allowing the supervisor to assign teams to the scene, hospital, detective bureau, etc.

☐ Confirm that all notifications have been made; for example, crime scene units, duty captain and/or supervisors, chiefs, sheriffs.

☐ Determine if additional staffing is needed to accomplish investigative goals.

☐ Upon arrival at the scene, determine if it is a static or dynamic scene and at what point the OIS investigators will assume control of the entire scene and investigation.

☐ Coordinate a briefing by on-scene personnel with investigators about what is known of the incident at that time, location of officer involved, witnesses, and steps taken to secure the scene, including any area where the scene was disturbed due to emergency or exigent circumstances. Secure dispatch tapes of entire incident, including all incoming calls and radio traffic, for follow-up investigative purposes.

☐ Ensure that a public information officer (PIO) or supervisor of administrative rank sets up a command post/media staging area and that no press release is made until sufficient information is available to ensure accuracy of information.

☐ Coordinate the investigation at the scene(s) and office to keep everyone apprised of information as it becomes available, including police broadcasts for additional suspects, etc.

Incident Scene Investigator(s)—Checklist

☐ Identify officer(s) involved.

☐ Identify any witnesses, civilian and department members; ensure that they are at a secure location and separated if possible.

☐ Ensure that the officer involved is removed from public and press scrutiny, and confirm that union peer representative is en route to his or her location.

☐ Depending on your agency's policies, the officer or employee should have trauma counselors or peer representatives to act as support for him or her during this extremely stressful period.

☐ Determine the boundaries of the scene, if possible, and ensure that the entire area is secured. A double-scene approach is preferable (Taped inner scene and barricaded or taped much larger outer scene to keep media and nonessential personnel away from forensic evidence.

☐ When investigators, crime scene personnel, and a supervisor of administrative rank have arrived, request that the officer involved or an employee witness accompany the investigative personnel through the scene, describing briefly how the OIS occurred. This provides investigators with the opportunity to determine the parameters of and information about the scene so they can organize the scene investigation.

Remember: A walk-through of the scene is of critical importance and should be completed by the officer or employee involved, if possible, or by an employee who witnessed the incident. It does not require actually walking

through the scene, risking the contamination of evidence; it merely requires that the employee stand at a location where he or she can point to critical areas and describe the incident. *Do not videotape*! The employee's ability to recall the incident in proper order may be affected by the extreme stress caused by the trauma of this shooting, and the chance of recounting an inaccurate chain of events could create unnecessary civil liabilities.

- [ ] It is advisable to photograph the employee(s) involved at the scene to show how he or she was attired at the time of the incident: plainclothes, uniform, visible police identification, caps or jackets with police logos, etc.
- [ ] It is not necessary to disarm the employee at the scene unless it is necessary for investigative purposes. The impounding of his or her weapon and countdown of ammunition should be away from public view.
- [ ] The employee can surrender his/her weapon at the station when he/she is issued a temporary-duty weapon.
- [ ] Depending on the circumstances of the incident, it may be necessary to impound the employee's gear and clothing for forensic analysis.
- [ ] Arrange to have witnesses and employee(s) involved transported separately to a location where they can be interviewed and taped statements obtained. Assign personnel to specifically care for these witnesses and ensure that their needs are addressed (phone calls, comfort, restrooms, etc.).
- [ ] All interviews should be taped, and the location of each witness in relation to the shooting scene should be documented due to witnesses seeing different things from different locations.

Interview of Employee(s) Involved

Remember: Never allow the employee involved to dictate his/her own report. The natural tendency to concentrate on the incident itself and not on the entire event requires that a statement be obtained and a total interview be conducted.

☐ The employee involved should be interviewed and notes taken after all other witnesses who are interviewed; the employee should then be released to crisis counselors and placed on administrative leave by his/her supervisor.

☐ A formal taped statement of the employee, in the presence of his or her immediate supervisor as well as a union representative and/or attorney, should be scheduled within 48 hours of the employee(s) actually using deadly force.

☐ Employees involved in traumatic events should be allowed time after their initial interview to calm down and gather their thoughts before a taped interview. This is established policy in many major police agencies.

☐ The trauma of the incident can cause the employee to forget the order in which the event occurred and critical portions of the OIS; giving the employee time to think will allow him/her to describe in detail his/her actions and those of the suspect(s).

☐ The immediate supervisor of the employee(s) involved shares a vicarious liability for any subordinates' actions; therefore, he/she should be directly involved in the interview process and aware of follow-up investigative findings.

Taped Interview of Employee(s) Involved

Due to the unique nature of each incident involving the use of deadly force, it is virtually impossible to make a list of questions that would be all inclusive; however, an investigator should allow the interviewee to describe in his/her own words how the armed confrontation occurred, then conduct an interview that covers all areas of the incident, including the state of mind of the officer involved at the time of the actual use of deadly force.

> *Remember*: **It is not necessary to Mirandize or provide Garrity (administrative)-type warnings in the investigative stages of a use-of-force investigation. Garrity warnings provide transactional immunity; Miranda warnings are custodial in nature.**

Follow-Up Investigation

- [ ] After completing the scene investigation and interviews of employee(s) involved along with any other police and civilian witnesses, it may be advisable to arrange for a videotaped walk-through with the employee(s) involved to be used in use-of-force boards and inquest-type reviews.
- [ ] OIS investigations are quite similar to homicide investigations, and depending on the circumstances of each incident, similar investigative steps should be taken.

Examples of investigative duties for OIS investigations include the following:

- [ ] Check adjacent businesses for witnesses
- [ ] Review incoming dispatch tapes for any persons reporting via cell phones
- [ ] Check area for any camera-equipped ATMs or store surveillance cameras
- [ ] Return to area at same approximate time of the incident and log license numbers to contact anyone who may travel through the area at the same time each day
- [ ] Set up informational roadblocks and pass out printed material concerning the OIS for public assistance
- [ ] Conduct a neighborhood canvass
- [ ] Publicize media releases
- [ ] Copy the video media coverage and watch for unknown witnesses who may have spoken to reporters but not to the police
- [ ] If the media filmed any portion of the incident, ask them for any raw unaired footage

Remember: **Approximately two-thirds of all households have video cameras and smart phones, so always look for individuals who may sell these tapes to the media. Be prepared to subpoena the original videos.**

Background Investigation

Suspect(s) and Witnesses

Do a complete background investigation on all suspects and parties involved, including the relationship, if any, of the witnesses to the participants. Document any gang affiliations and/or factions, and obtain criminal records.

Employee(s)

- ☐ Obtain a copy of the training history and duty assignments of the employee(s) involved, and attach them to their statements.
- ☐ If the employee(s) involved has worked for other police agencies, make sure his or her work history and experience are properly documented.
- ☐ Has the employee been involved in other OISs or use-of-force incidents? Dispositions?

Preparation of Investigative Report

A comprehensive report which depicts the entire event is of critical importance.

- A. Preparation
  - ☐ Upon obtaining transcribed copies of all taped statements and communications tapes, complete a use-of-force investigation administrative report.
- B. Chronological narrative
  - ☐ Document location of occurrence, and date and time of incident.
  - ☐ Identify employee(s) involved, including witness employees.
  - ☐ Describe the type and nature of deadly force used.
  - ☐ Describe scene, including background areas (field of fire, lighting conditions, etc.).
  - ☐ Note employee's duty assignment (plainclothes, uniform, unmarked or marked police vehicles)?

☐ Identify weapons involved by make, model, serial number, and caliber.

☐ Confirm whether weapon was duty, off-duty, or backup.

☐ Confirm that weapon was departmentally issued or authorized, and ammunition used was also authorized or issued.

C. Deceased or living suspect?

☐ Identify any and all suspects involved in this incident, including the following:

1. Complete physical description
2. Prior criminal history
3. Parole or probation status
4. Known associates (possible witnesses)
5. If deceased, autopsy or cause of death
6. If injured, describe injuries, including hospital and attending physician information.
7. If charged, detail charges pending prosecution.

D. Witnesses

☐ Describe all witnesses, and provide a brief summary of what they observed.

1. Name, address, and telephone number
2. Complete physical description, D.O.B., SS#
3. Witnesses' location at time of incident, and their observations
4. Their relationship, if any, to any of the participants

Remember: **All use-of-force or OIS situations are different; this interview format is merely a guide regarding areas of concern that should be addressed when interviewing employees or officers involved in a very stressful situation.**

Appendix: Procedures for the Collection of Evidence

The proper collection and disposition of evidence will be accomplished if these guidelines are followed

- ☐ Each piece of evidence should be marked (on the container or item as applicable) to show its original position and location. This information should also be recorded in the investigator's notebook.
- ☐ Each piece of evidence should be photographed prior to being placed in an appropriate sealed evidence container.
- ☐ Each article should be marked distinctively by the searching officer to identify the person who found the particular piece of evidence. In cases of small or fluid specimens, this marking is done on the container.
- ☐ Each item should be described exactly and completely, with the corresponding case numbers affixed and the date and time of collection indicated.
- ☐ Each item should be packaged in a separate, clean, and properly sized container to prevent cross-contamination or damage.
- ☐ Each package should be sealed to retain evidence and prevent any unauthorized handling.
  - ☐ If evidence can be considered a biohazard, the outside of the packaging should clearly note this.
  - ☐ If evidence is to be examined for the presence of latent prints, the outside of the packaging should clearly note this.
  - ☐ If evidence is to be examined for the presence of DNA, the outside of the packaging should clearly note this.
  - ☐ If a firearm cannot be safely rendered safe (empty of cartridges), arrangements should be made to hand carry it to the police laboratory or crime lab facility. Never package and ship a loaded firearm.
- ☐ Each piece of evidence should show proper disposition:
  1. Police department laboratory
  2. Property clerk's office
  3. FBI laboratory

☐ Proper records should be kept regarding each piece of evidence showing chain of custody. These records should reflect any movement of the evidence from the point of origin to its final disposition.

Collection of Specific Types of Evidence

The homicide investigator is usually confronted with the same general types of evidence in most murder investigations, such as blood, bullets, and fingerprints. The evidence ordinarily falls within three distinct categories: *objects*, *body materials*, and *impressions* (see table below).

Examples of Physical Evidence		
Objects	*Body materials*	*Impressions*
Weapons	Blood	Fingerprints
Tools	Semen	Tire tracks
Firearms	Hair	Footprints
Displaced furniture	Tissue	Palm Prints
Notes, letters or papers	Spittle	Tool marks
Bullets	Urine	Bullet holes
Vehicles	Feces	Newly damaged areas
Cigarette/cigar butts	Vomit	Dents and breaks

Body Materials

Blood (Wet)

Large Amounts or Pools

☐ Use a disposable eyedropper or hypodermic syringe to collect the fluid, and transfer it to a sterile container (5 cc is sufficient for testing purposes).

☐ Transfer immediately to laboratory or refrigerate specimen. However, *do not freeze blood*.

☐ In some instances, depending on the jurisdiction's regulations, a chemical preservative such as sodium azide or ethylenediaminetetraacetic acid (EDTA) can be used to prevent blood spoilage.

☐ Only perform this procedure if you have been trained to do so.

Small Amounts

- ☐ Use a 100% cotton swab, #8 cotton thread, or sterile gauze pad to collect specimen.
- ☐ Allow swab, thread, or gauze pad to air dry.
- ☐ Place in sterile test tube or other clean container.

Bloodstains (Dry)

Nonporous Surface

- ☐ If there is a sufficient amount of dry blood, it can be scraped from the surface with a clean, disposable razor blade or sterile scalpel.
- ☐ These scrapings should be shaved into a sterile container.

Porous Surface (Fabric, Unfinished Wood, etc.)

- ☐ Collect and submit the article containing the stain to the laboratory as found.
- ☐ Wrap in separate and sterile container. If the article is too large or inappropriate to transport, remove a portion of the material containing an adequate amount of the stain for transport to the laboratory for analysis.

Traces or Smears That Cannot Be Scraped into Container

- ☐ Moisten a 100% cotton swab or sterile gauze pad with distilled water. Also obtain a control sample that should be forwarded to the lab for analysis with the specimen.
- ☐ Place swab or pad on stain and allow stain to soften and soak into swab or gauze pad.
- ☐ Allow to air dry.
- ☐ Place into a sterile test tube or container for laboratory.

Semen

The following techniques should be employed at the scene.

Semen Wet Stain

- ☐ Swab or wash (by medical examiner, if possible).
- ☐ Draw the fluid into a disposable eyedropper or hypodermic syringe.
- ☐ Place in sterile test tube.
- ☐ Use swab or sterile cotton gauze pad for samples of smaller quantities which are still moist.
- ☐ Allow to air dry immediately, and place in sterile container.

Semen Dry Stain

- ☐ Dry stain will have a stiff, "starchy" texture.
- ☐ If it is on clothing, submit the entire article, being careful not to break or contaminate the stained area.
- ☐ If it is on the body, using 100% cotton sterile gauze pad moistened with distilled water, gently remove stain and place in sterile test tube or other clean container after allowing it to air dry.

Urine

- ☐ Remove by disposable eyedropper or sterile gauze pad.
- ☐ Place in sterile test tube or other clean container.
- ☐ If on clothing, the entire article should be submitted.

Spittle or Saliva

- ☐ Remove with disposable eyedropper or 100% cotton sterile gauze pad.
- ☐ Place in sterile test tube or other clean container after drying. Mark as biohazard.

Feces

Large Amount

- ☐ Remove with a small clean shovel. Allow to air dry.
- ☐ Place in sterile container. Mark storage container as biohazard.

Small Amount

- ☐ Remove with 100% cotton sterile swab or gauze pad moistened with distilled water, then air dry or scrape into container.
- ☐ Place in sterile test tube. Mark as biohazard.

Vomit

- ☐ Remove with eyedropper or small shovel depending on amount.
- ☐ Place into sterile container. Mark as biohazard.

It should be noted that any physiological fluid found at the scene, such as urine, saliva, feces, perspiration, ear wax, nasal mucus, can be typed into the same grouping as blood, provided the material comes from an individual who is a secretor.

Furthermore, DNA testing can be performed to identify the suspect who left these materials behind.

Tissue

- ☐ Remove with tweezers.
- ☐ Place in a clean glass container or sterile test tube.
- ☐ Forward to the medical examiner. Mark as biohazard.

Hair

It is recommended that a sample of hair from various parts of the body be obtained in all homicide cases. Even though hair evidence may not be crucial or known to exist in the early stages of the investigation, it may be discovered later, even after the body has been buried or destroyed through cremation.

- ☐ Samples should always be taken from various parts by pulling or plucking so as to obtain a piece of the root. If pulling or plucking absolutely cannot be undertaken for some reason, cutting the hair close to the scalp will suffice.

☐ An ordinary sampling will comprise approximately 24–48 pieces of hair. Hair removed from the head should be taken as follows: front, back, left side, right side, and top.

☐ The sample roots should then be air dried.

Collection of Hairs from the Scene

Using oblique lighting, scan the surfaces of the crime scene.

☐ If hairs or fibers are located, gather by tweezers, being careful not to bend or break.

☐ Masking tape or Scotch tape can be used to gather small fibers or hairs.

☐ Place in sterile container and seal. (Folded paper or envelopes may also be used.)

The table below discusses the use of DNA technology for bodily fluids and bones.

Application of DNA Technology

Blood (White Cells)	
Liquid	1–100 μL (microliters)
	Size of a quarter
	One drop
Preservation	EDTA (purple cap) refrigeration
Dried	Approximately the size of a dime
Preservation	Keep dry, and refrigerate or freeze.

Semen	
Liquid	1–20 μL (microliters)
	Approximately the size of a dime
Preservation	Add EDTA and refrigerate
Dried	Requires a sufficient amount of sperm
Preservation	Keep dry, and refrigerate or freeze.
	Laboratory—separate sperm.

Urine	
Cellular material	10,000 cells (approximately 60 ml)
Liquid	60–100 cc (approximately 2 oz)
	Isolate cellular material.
	Freeze (–70° C).
Dried	Keep dry and freeze.

Saliva	
Buccal cells	10,000 cells (one drop)
Liquid	Separate buccal cells, dry, and freeze.
Dried	Keep dry, and refrigerate or freeze.

Tissues (Bones)	
Minimum amount	100–500 mg (1 in.)
Fresh	Freeze (–70°C).
Dried	Keep dry and freeze.

DNA profiling can be utilized to (1) establish the link between evidential DNA and the possible suspect's DNA; and (2) identify whether the DNA in question is human or nonhuman, and establish the sex of the origin.

Objects

Bullets

- ☐ Bullets should be collected without damaging or marking the *rifling*.
- ☐ Bullets embedded in doors, trees, walls, etc. should be removed by taking out a portion of the object in which the bullet has become lodged rather than by probing or digging. Digging for the bullet may cause additional marks which may destroy the ballistics value of the evidence.
- ☐ Recovered bullets should be examined for blood or other materials before packaging.
- ☐ Bullets should be marked on the base or nose.
- ☐ Each bullet should be packaged separately in an appropriate container, preferably one which will prevent any cross-contamination or accidental abrasion of the rifling marks.
- ☐ Package should be marked to show identification and location of discovery.

Discharged Casings or Cartridges

- ☐ Recovered casings should be marked on the inside wall of the shell by the mouth end, or, if this is not possible, as close to the opening as possible.
- ☐ Never mark the recovered casing on or near the end which contained the primer cap, because examination of weapon markings may be destroyed.
- ☐ Always consider the possibility of fingerprints on the sides of these casings, and take appropriate methods to preserve them.
- ☐ Package in separate containers with proper documentation.
- ☐ If casing was photographed, in situ, with a crime scene marker, note the number or letter of the photo.

Shotgun Shells

- ☐ Plastic or paper shotgun shells should be handled in the same manner as other discharged casings.
- ☐ These items can be marked on the metal side part of the casing.
- ☐ *Never mark on base of shell casing.*

Live Cartridges or Rounds of Ammunition

- ☐ Examine for fingerprint evidence prior to marking.
- ☐ Mark on side of casing.
- ☐ Package, indicating the location of recovered rounds.
- ☐ Mark packaging: "LIVE AMMUNITION."

Shotgun Wadding

- ☐ Recover and submit for laboratory examination.
- ☐ Place in a separate container.

Weapons

- ☐ Photograph and examine for fingerprints.
- ☐ Examine for any serology or other trace evidence.
- ☐ Determine if the weapon is to be examined for DNA. Most crime lab facilities have a hierarchy for examining weapons for presence of DNA.
- ☐ Place in special container according to the weapon's size to protect evidence and prevent handling.
- ☐ If evidence is to be examined for the presence of DNA, the outside packaging should clearly note this.
- ☐ Forward to serology or crime lab for further analysis.

Firearms

- ☐ Photograph in original position.
- ☐ Most crime lab facilities have a hierarchy for examining weapons for presence of DNA.
- ☐ Examine for fingerprints *ONLY* if a DNA examination will *NOT* be conducted.

☐ Examine for any serology (e.g., blowback of close-range firing may result in blood, hair, or tissue being transferred to weapon or into barrel of weapon).

☐ Upon completion of preliminary examination (see previous list items), unload weapon and render it safe before transporting it.

☐ Package firearm individually in an appropriate container. In circumstances in which the firearm must be transported for further examination at a proper facility, use a cardboard box. Draw a string through the trigger guard and attach this string at either end of the box, leaving the gun in a suspended position. For larger firearms such as rifles or shotguns, cut a notch in each end of the box and lay weapon across container.

☐ Indicate the brand name, model designation, serial numbers, caliber, and number of shots the weapon is capable of firing, e.g., 5- or 6-shot revolver, in reports and on evidence containers. Also indicate the type of finish, e.g., nickel plate.

☐ All weapons recovered should be marked for identification as soon as possible in the following manner:
 1. Revolvers—mark on frame, barrel, and cylinder.
 2. Rifles and shotguns—mark on receiver, bolt, and barrel.
 3. Semiautomatic weapons—mark on receiver (frame), slide, barrel, and any magazines.

Fibers

Fibers, such as hairs, may be transferred between the victim and perpetrator and may provide the investigator with an additional piece of class evidence which can be subjected to microscopic and microchemical testing. Items such as fibers, rope, string, and twine should be collected for examination.

☐ Collect fibers as follows:
 1. Use forceps or tweezers
 2. Tape
 3. Vacuum sweeping (It should be noted that this is the least desirable method because too many contaminants are also collected.)

- [ ] Collecting samples by using the sticky side of tape is considered the most practical method.
- [ ] Place samples from each area gathered in individual containers, mark appropriately, and forward to laboratory for examination.

Fabric

Pieces of fabric found at the scene can be examined in a manner similar to fiber to determine:

- [ ] Color
- [ ] Type of cloth and fiber
- [ ] Thread count
- [ ] Direction of fiber twist
- [ ] Dye

Class as well as individual characteristics can be obtained from fragments of fabric when matched by physically fitting evidence pieces into their source.

Clothing

Each item of clothing collected as evidence should be individually wrapped in order to prevent cross-contamination. If the clothing to be collected is wet, it should be air dried before it is packaged. Clothing may provide the investigator with additional evidence:

- [ ] Examine all articles with the naked eye first, and then reexamine using an alternate light source (ALS).
- [ ] Stains on clothing may match stains from the scene, the victim, or the suspect.
- [ ] The victim's clothing may contain saliva and/or seminal fluid from the perpetrator.
- [ ] Hairs or fibers may be present on clothing that match similar hairs or fibers from a particular scene or location or from the victim.

- [ ] Tears or cuts in clothing made by the weapon can be matched to show the position of the victim at the time of assault.
- [ ] The deposit of gunshot residues on clothing can be analyzed to determine the approximate distance from which the gun was fired.

Cigarette or Cigar Butts

Cigarette or cigar butts found at the crime scene, especially those with filter tips, can be examined by serologists for the determination of blood type and sometimes other genetic factors (e.g., sex) of individuals who are secretors. (See also in the *Practical Homicide Investigation* textbook, Chapter 16, "Application of DNA Analysis," page 533.)

- [ ] Collect with sterile forceps or tweezers and ensure dryness.
- [ ] Place into separate containers to prevent contamination.
- [ ] Containers should be appropriately marked.
- [ ] Forward to serology.
- [ ] If evidence is to be examined for the presence of DNA, the outside of the packaging should clearly note this.

Displaced Furniture

- [ ] Examine for any fingerprints or serology.
- [ ] Useful in crime reconstruction.

Insects

A variety of insects on the remains and at the crime scene are invaluable in determining the approximate time of death, or postmortem interval (PMI). Human DNA has been successfully extracted from larvae and used to link victim to crime scene, victim to weapon, and weapon to crime scene.

- [ ] A sampling of insects should be recovered from the crime scene before the body is removed and transported to the morgue.
- [ ] If possible, photograph the insects *in situ* from a discreet distance, as blowflies and carrion beetles tend to move away when the presence of humans is detected.

☐ If a sampling of insects cannot be done at the crime scene or in the field, the body bag holding the remains should be clearly marked for the examining pathologist that live insects are enclosed and should be collected from the remains for entomological examination, prior to the remains being cleaned and prepped for autopsy.

Common Insects Found on Human Remains and at Crime Scenes

☐ Blowflies, associated maggot larvae, and their respective pupae. They are considered the most important flies pertaining to forensic entomology.
☐ House flies
☐ Carrion beetles
☐ Rove beetles
☐ Ants
☐ Wasps
☐ Cockroaches

Investigative Considerations

☐ DNA extracted from the gastrointestinal tracts of maggots can be used to identify the deceased person, even though the remains may not be identifiable. The DNA in the maggots can be matched to the DNA of the deceased.
☐ Note: Cockroach bites when observed on deceased infants can be instrumental when trying to prove long-term instances of child abuse against a parent, caretaker, or guardian.
☐ The presence of an insect not indigenous to the geography where the remains are discovered may indicate the remains were transported from another portion of the country.
☐ Some insects will appear only at certain seasons of the year.
☐ There is a progressive order of insect arrival and activity: One particular insect will not arrive and begin its work until the prior insects

have departed after completing their part in the decomposition process.

Equipment

- [ ] Hand net, for trapping flying insects
- [ ] Sterile or disposable forceps
- [ ] Hand shovel or digging tools
- [ ] Sterile jars, vials, and plastic sealable bags
- [ ] 70% isopropyl alcohol
- [ ] Thermometer
- [ ] Climatological data: present time and temperature of remains, and internal temperature of room where remains are located or external temperature of scene if remains are located outdoors
- [ ] Historical climatic data of area in which the remains were located

Procedures

- [ ] Collect live specimens from the remains (blowflies, maggots, beetles, etc.). Preserve a portion of the specimens in sterile vials containing 70% isopropyl alcohol. Also place a live sampling of specimens in a sterile jar with holes in the lid to avoid suffocation and death. Note where specimens were obtained, time, and temperature.
- [ ] Collect dead specimens from the remains such as pupae, hard shell casings, or cocoons of larvae. Place specimens in a sterile jar or vial.
- [ ] Collect live specimens from the area surrounding the remains, up to several feet, if needed (blowflies, maggots, beetles, etc.). Preserve a portion of specimens in sterile vials containing 70% isopropyl alcohol. Also place a live sampling of specimens in a sterile jar with holes in the lid to avoid suffocation and death. Note where specimens were obtained, time, and temperature.
- [ ] Collect dead specimens from the area surrounding the remains (up to several feet, if needed), such as pupae, hard shell casings, or cocoons of larvae. Place specimens in a sterile jar or vial.
- [ ] Finally, repeat the collection process above, after the remains have been removed from the scene, noting the time and temperature.

☐ Contact the forensic entomologist who will be examining your insects and related material for instructions on shipping procedures, type of forensic analysis to be undertaken, and results hoped to be obtained.

Soil

Collection of Soil Samples

☐ Collect several samples at the scene from various locations because mineral and organic contents vary within short distances.

☐ Gather at least a cupful or handful from each location.

☐ Ensure dryness.

☐ Package in separate containers.

☐ Mark properly for identification and location.

Tools

Tools which are suspected of having been used in the crime should be examined as follows:

☐ Examine for serology or fingerprints.

☐ If the tool contains any serological or DNA evidence, it must be carefully packaged to preserve this evidence.

☐ If evidence is to be examined for the presence of DNA, the outside of the packaging should clearly note this.

☐ If tool contains traces of certain materials that are to be matched up with known samples, care must be taken so that this material is not rubbed off.

☐ Portion of tool to be matched must be protected.

☐ Broken tools and/or knives can be fracture-matched to provide positive identification.

☐ *Never try to fit tool into tool mark or match broken pieces together.*

Vehicles

If found recently abandoned, consider enlisting the aid of personnel with trained canines to search for the occupants.

- ☐ Photograph and examine for serology or DNA evidence.
- ☐ Process for fingerprints, only if no DNA is present.
- ☐ Examine for other items of evidence.
- ☐ Search for weapons.
- ☐ Examine the vehicle's navigation system (Global Positioning System, or GPS), if so equipped, for
  - ☐ Recent travel
  - ☐ Home location
  - ☐ Favorite destinations
  - ☐ Recent locations traveled

Documents (Letters, Notes, and Papers)

These items may be examined to ascertain authenticity, locate fingerprints, or determine authorship in suicide cases, or for more advanced techniques (see *Practical Homicide Investigation*).

- ☐ The primary consideration in handling this type of evidence is the preservation of any fingerprints which may be on the item.
- ☐ Evidence should be collected by using disposable tweezers or forceps to gently pick up the paper.
- ☐ Each item should be placed in a separate package. A package which is clear or see-through is best since it will allow the investigator to examine contents without contaminating the document with additional fingerprints.
- ☐ If see-through packages are not available, the object can be photocopied using forceps to place the object on the machine and later to transfer it to the evidence envelope. (This will allow for reading and other examination of content without disturbing the evidence value of the original document.) The documents may be digitally photographed.

☐ Marking this type of evidence depends on the type of examination to be conducted. In some instances, a mark can be placed on a back corner of the paper. In other instances, just the package in which the document is placed will be marked.
☐ Documents should not be folded.
☐ Examine for latent prints.
☐ Saliva on envelopes may contain DNA in sufficient amounts that a DNA profile may be developed.
☐ Saliva on envelopes can also be examined for sex origin.
☐ If the evidence is to be examined for the presence of DNA, the outside packaging should clearly note this.

Glass

Glass should be collected as follows:

☐ Small pieces should be placed in a vial or pillbox.
☐ Large pieces should be placed in a sturdy cardboard box with proper padding or protection to prevent further breakage during transport.
☐ In cases involving broken headlamps or taillights from automobiles, it should be ascertained and documented as to whether the light switches in the car were in the on or off position when the vehicle was discovered.

Impressions

Fingerprint Examination

It should be noted that fingerprint powders *do not* interfere with serological analyses. However, ninhydrin sprays and other chemical means to make prints visible may interfere with serology tests.

Types of Fingerprints

Fingerprints are divided into three separate categories:

Plastic prints: These impressions occur when the finger touches or presses against a soft pliable surface such as putty, gum, a newly painted area, the glue on a stamp or envelope, wax, flour, thick dust, soap, grease, tar, resin, or clay. A negative impression of the friction ridge pattern is produced, resulting in a *plastic print.*

Visible prints: These prints occur when the fingers, palms, or feet which have been contaminated with a foreign substance come into contact with a clean surface and are pressed onto the surface, leaving a print. The most common type is the dust print. However, substances such as ink, blood, soot, paint, grease, face powders, and oils contaminate the friction ridges of the fingers; when they are pressed against another surface, an image is transferred.

Latent prints: These prints occur from natural skin secretions such as perspiration. When grease or dirt is mixed with the natural secretions, a stable print may be deposited on the surface. Latent prints, which are not visible, are usually found on objects with smooth or polished surfaces or on paper.

The latent print is developed by a dusting or chemical process. In some instances, these latent prints can be developed on rougher surfaces by using certain chemical processes.

Development of Fingerprints

The most common and practical method of developing prints at crime scenes is through the "dusting" technique. This is done by dusting or spreading fingerprint powder with a brush over the surface of the object suspected of bearing prints. The most common color powders are black, silver, gray, and white. However, fingerprint powders come in many other colors which can be used to contrast with any background. The brushes available are composed of camel's hair, feather dusters, fiberglass, or nylon.

> ***Note***: **Use a digital camera and lens combination, which allows for a 1×1 rendering or life-sized photo of the fingerprint before lifting.**

☐ A small amount of powder is poured onto a clean piece of paper.

☐ The brush is drawn across the powder and then tapped with the finger to remove excess material.

☐ The surface of object to be searched is then lightly brushed by the investigator, who uses curved strokes to locate prints.

Another method of dusting is done with magnetic powders. The Magna Brush is dipped into the magnetic powder, which then adheres to the magnet in the brush. When the powder, which is actually fine iron fillings, is evenly distributed on the end of the brush, the investigator uses the applicator like any other fingerprint brush.

It should be noted that in addition to latent fingerprints, palmar (palm and wrist) or plantar (foot and toe) skin designs may be found at the scene.

Chemical Processes

In addition to the powders, there are a series of chemical procedures which can be employed to develop latent prints. These are iodine fuming, ninhydrin, and silver nitrate. Furthermore, some remarkable results have occurred in developing latent prints by use of a laser. Practically speaking, the average investigator will not be employing these procedures. However, one should be aware of the availability of these methods in the event that further examination of evidence is necessary in order to discover and develop latent print evidence.

Tire Tracks and Footprints

These impressions may be left in various types of material. The footprint is the most common impression left at or near the scene of a crime. Impressions should be collected in the following manner:

☐ *Photograph*: Prior to photography, the impression should be cleaned of all foreign matter. Lighting should be employed so as to enhance the details. A scale of measure should be included in the photo. Then a long-range view and a close-up should be taken.

☐ *Casting*: A casting kit should be available for use at the crime scene which contains the following materials:

1. Plaster of Paris (5 pounds)
2. Mixing container (flexible for reuse)
3. Stirring stick
4. Reinforcement material (sticks, wire, etc., to hold form)
5. Shellac or plastic spray (to fix soft earth or dust)
6. Oil spray (to serve as a release agent)

Preparation for Casting

- ☐ Clean out the loose material without disturbing the impression.
- ☐ Use plastic spray to fix soil prior to pouring plaster.
- ☐ Build a form around impression to avoid runoff.
- ☐ Gently pour plaster of Paris over impression.
- ☐ Add reinforcement sticks as form builds.

Preservation of Dust Prints

- ☐ Photograph first.
- ☐ Use a special lifter (black rubber with a sticky surface) placed sticky-side down over impression. Press on the impression, then remove lifter.

Tool Marks

Tool marks, as footprints and tire tracks, may contain minute imperfections which are unique and can sometimes be microscopically compared to a tool or object in question. It is better if the investigator can remove the object which bears the tool mark. This can be done by removing the surface for submission to the laboratory. In instances where this would be impractical, the tool mark can be cast with a silicone rubber material. To collect a tool mark:

- ☐ Photograph (long-shot and close-up) with a digital camera and lens combination, which allows a 1 × 1 exposure or renders a life-sized photo.
- ☐ Cast with a silicone rubber casting after spraying surface with silicone release agent.

Newly Damaged Areas

The presence of damaged furniture or objects, and any other newly damaged areas, may be indicative of some sort of violence or struggle.

- ☐ Photograph.
- ☐ Examine with naked eye for DNA-type materials such as blood, semen, and saliva.
- ☐ Reexamine with an alternate light source (ALS). These can be the portable handheld models or the larger high-powered types which require an AC power source.
- ☐ Process for fingerprints.
- ☐ Attempt to determine just where furniture or objects may have been located prior to the acts of violence and/or struggle. This will aid in reenacting or reconstructing the crime scene.

Collection of Bite-Mark Evidence at the Scene

The proper handling of bite-mark evidence begins at the scene of the crime, where the homicide detective must initiate procedures to ensure that it is not destroyed or lost.

I recommend that the investigator take photographs of any pattern of injury he or she observes on the body while at the scene, giving special attention to any ovoid-shaped wounds or marks which are less than 2 inches in diameter. The following procedures at the crime scene are recommended.

Photographs of the Bite-Mark Wound

- ☐ Use a digital camera and lens combination, which allows a 1×1 exposure or renders a life-sized photo of the wound (see Figure 43).

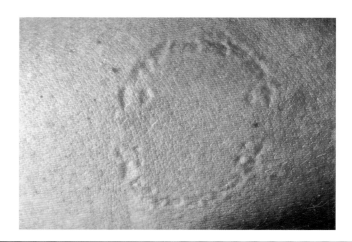

FIGURE 43 Photo of bite mark prior to processing. 1 x 1 exposure which renders a lifesize photo of the wound. Courtesy of Detective Mark Czworniak, Chicago, Illinois Police Department. Permission from Vernon Geberth, *Practical Homicide Investigation: Tactics, Procedures, and Forensic Techniques*, 4th ed. (Boca Raton, FL: CRC Press, 2006), 131.

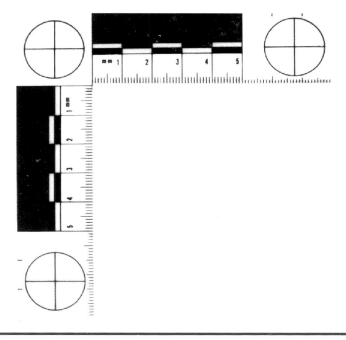

FIGURE 44 An ABO#2 bite-mark scale.

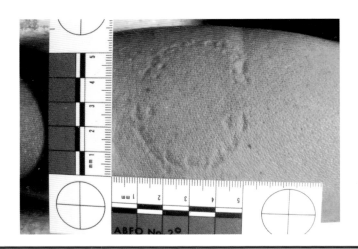

FIGURE 45   When measuring bite marks, use a rule of measure in the photo to document size, preferably an ABO#2 bite-mark scale. Courtesy of Detective Mark Czworniak, Chicago, Illinois Police Department. Permission from Vernon Geberth, *Practical Homicide Investigation: Tactics, Procedures, and Forensic Techniques*, 4th ed. (Boca Raton, FL: CRC Press, 2006), 131.

☐ Use a rule of measure, preferably an ABO#2 bite-mark scale (see Figure 44), in the photo to document size. The ruler which is used should not be white in color because white is not conducive to enhancement (see example of ruler in Figures 44 and 45).

☐ Use oblique lighting to enhance bite mark.

☐ Provide for an anatomical landmark in photo.

☐ Take photos in black-and-white and in color.

☐ Take an overall photo and a close-up, at the 1×1 setting of each wound.

☐ Do not delete any "bad" shots, but save all digital files and photos. They are evidence.

Saliva Washings

☐ Take a saliva washing of the bite-mark area for DNA analysis or blood grouping and serological examination.

☐ Washing should be done with distilled water and 100% cotton. Start at the periphery, and work inward; use a separate swab for each bite mark. (If there is no distilled water available, use tap water, but take a control sample for examination.)

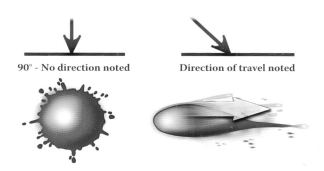

90° - No direction noted   Direction of travel noted

FIGURE 46 Blood spatters with (left) no direction noted and (right) direction clearly noted. Illustration courtesy of Brian Wilson, Medical Legal Art, © 2007, www.doereport.com.

- ☐ Air-dry each swab.
- ☐ Place each swab in a separate container, preferably a sterile test tube.
- ☐ Take a saliva swab from the victim for a control sample.
- ☐ Take a control swab from an area of the body other than the bite mark.
- ☐ Label each sample; keep the items separate.

Remember: **Always keep track of the chain of custody.**

Bloodstain Pattern Analysis (Examination of Blood Spatter)

The investigator should have a working knowledge of examining bloodstains and patterns at a crime scene. The actual stringing and analysis of bloodstain patterns should be performed by a certified expert, if your intentions are to admit this type of evidence into a criminal trial. (See Figure 46.)

Investigative Considerations

- ☐ Observations of the type, quantity, and locations of bloodstains and how they got there will allow you to reconstruct what took place in the scene.
- ☐ A properly documented crime scene with notes, sketches, measurements, and photographs will allow a trained bloodstain pattern analyst to properly interpret events.

- [ ] A basic understanding of how blood arrives at Point B from Point A can help in determining:
  - [ ] What is type of death: homicide, suicide, accidental, or natural?
  - [ ] Is this a *staged crime scene*?
  - [ ] What type of instrument was used to inflict the injuries resulting in the blood patterns?
  - [ ] Do all the bloodstains come from the same sources?
  - [ ] In what direction was the victim and/or offender traveling?
  - [ ] Where was the victim when the injuries were sustained?
  - [ ] Where was the offender?

Crime Scene Examination

- [ ] Wear the proper protective garments: Tyvex, shoe covers, latex gloves.

  Remember: **Blood and blood byproducts, saliva, semen, urine, and feces are biohazards.**

- [ ] Carefully enter the crime scene, taking care to observe what is on the floor or ground in front of you so that you don't contaminate the bloodstains.
- [ ] Look up, down, and all around.
- [ ] Examine and process only one room at a time.
- [ ] Make notes of the locations of any bloodstains.
- [ ] Ensure that they are photographed and measured before they are damaged.

Crime Scene Documentation

- [ ] Your documentation of the scene should include field notes; measurements of distance, angle, and sizes; sketching; and photographs.
- [ ] Prepare a sketch of your crime scene, and document on your sketch where the blood patterns appear.
- [ ] Document the floor first and then the walls. Work on one wall at a time.
- [ ] Once the sketches of your rooms are completed, begin to photograph the bloodstain patterns.

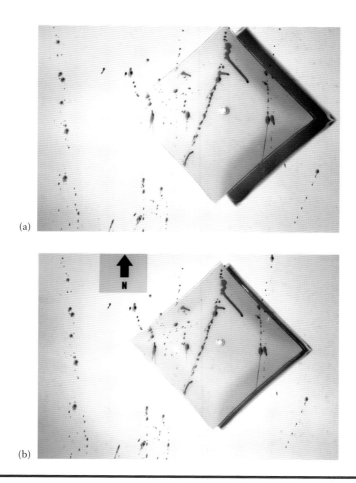

(a)

(b)

FIGURE 47   **Blood spatter evidence.** These photos illustrate the proper documentation and photography of blood spatter evidence on the ceiling light fixture. Photo (a) Before adding the reference marker. Photo (b) with the marker. Courtesy of Detective Mark Czworniak, Chicago, Illinois Police Department. Permission from Vernon Geberth, *Practical Homicide Investigation: Tactics, Procedures, and Forensic Techniques*, 4th ed. (Boca Raton, FL: CRC Press, 2006), 201.

☐ Use of a tripod should always be considered and utilized when photographing bloodstains.

☐ The crime scene should be photographed before the introduction of any rulers, scales, or markers.

☐ If using a digital camera, use the highest resolution setting available.

Figure 47 gives examples of documenting and photographing blood spatter evidence.

Crime Scene Collection of Electronic and Digital Evidence

Investigative Considerations

☐ The investigator must first determine the legal authority of search and seizure in federal and state statutes and local laws as they apply to electronic evidence. In addition, the investigator must understand the fragile nature of electronic evidence and the principles and procedures associated with its collection and preservation.

Identification of Digital Evidence

☐ Digital evidence can reside in a variety of different formats: e-mails, digital photographs, ATM transaction logs, word-processing documents, instant message histories, files saved from accounting programs, spreadsheets, Internet browser histories, databases, computer printouts, GPS tracks, logs from a hotel's electronic door locks, digital video audio files.

☐ Digital evidence can reside on a variety of different devices: desktop, laptop, or notebook computers as well as smartphones. The contents of computer memory can be stored in both internal and external hard drives, thumb drives (USB), also known as removable media. These types of devices can be as small as a dime and easily hidden or disguised. The following should also be examined for possible evidence: computer backup devices; Internet servers (on- or offsite); memory cards (memory sticks, SD cards, micro SD cards, compact flash, and XD); recordable optical media, such as CDs, DVDs, Blu-Ray DVDs, VHS cassettes, and music cassettes; smartphones, standard cellular telephones, and landline telephones with answering machines and caller ID features; tablet devices, music storage devices (e.g., iPods and MP3 players); personal data assistants (PDA); digital voice recorders; television digital video recorders (DVRs); floppy discs; tape backup devices; Zip drive media; and cloud storage services.

Additional Investigative Considerations

- ☐ It is important to note that potential evidence may be lost or destroyed if a running computer is encountered by law enforcement, seized as part of an investigation, and removed from its power source.
- ☐ Whether or not a computer or device is powered up will determine how it should be seized. When in doubt, contact a trained forensic computer examiner.

Volatile Data Collection Strategy for Powered-Up Computers

- ☐ Document all actions conducted on a running machine.
- ☐ Photograph the screen of the running system to document its state.
- ☐ Identify the operating system running on the suspect machine.
- ☐ Note date and time, if shown on screen, and record with the current actual time.
- ☐ Dump the RAM from the system to external storage source.

Computers

Collection Procedures

- ☐ Arrangements should always be prearranged as to who will be examining the computers or devices once they are recovered.
- ☐ If an offender or suspect is present in the area where the seized devices are located, remove him or her from the area to prevent the destruction of potential evidence. Computers can be programmed to wipe the hard drive clean in a matter of seconds.
- ☐ If the device is off, do not power it on.
- ☐ If the device is on, leave it on until it can be photographed. Photographs should be taken of the screen, and any peripheral equipment, including how interconnecting cables are attached to the devices.

☐ Do not attempt to access the contents of the computer or device unless an emergency situation exists.

☐ Be aware that once the device is powered off, it may require a password to access the data when powered on again. Attempt to locate any manuals or notes which may list passwords.

☐ If the device is connected to a battery-operated backup system, remove the device from AC power and transport both the device and the battery backup to your facility, where the backup device can be plugged back into an AC outlet.

☐ If the device is a laptop computer, ascertain if the battery is fully charged before transporting it. Ensure that all power supplies and cables are seized along with the device.

☐ If multiple computers or devices exist, document where the equipment was found and what peripherals were seized with each device.

☐ Label all cables, and record which devices they connect.

☐ Recover any charging cradles or power supplies for the device or any peripherals.

☐ Disconnect any Ethernet cables for network and Internet access from the wall outlet.

☐ If a wireless router or cable modem is present, remove it from the power supply. Collect the cable modem and cables as well.

☐ Adequately prepare the equipment to safeguard from shock and damage prior to removal and transport.

☐ Identify proprietary software.

☐ If the device is an in-dash navigation system (GPS), it is often best to seize the entire vehicle rather than attempt to remove the GPS from the dashboard.

Cellular Phones

Investigative Considerations

As with computers and related devices, cellular telephones can provide a wealth of evidence and information. Prior to seizing and examining a cellular telephone, the investigator should be familiar with all related federal and state statutes and local laws, relative to search and seizure, prior to collecting and examining any electronic evidence.

- [ ] Much of the same digital evidence that can be found on a computer can also be stored on a cellular telephone.
- [ ] Some cellular telephones can provide an accurate GPS of where the phone has recently traveled.
- [ ] Decide whether the phone will be examined for fingerprint evidence or biological evidence.
- [ ] If the phone is off, leave it off. Collect any related charging cradles or power supplies. Unplug any power supplies, and determine if the power supply connects with the particular phone you are collecting.
  - [ ] If the phone has a removable SIMM card, remove it, and document its removal.
  - [ ] If the phone has a removable micro SD card, remove it, and document its removal.
- [ ] If the phone is on, leave it on.
  - [ ] Photograph the contents of the screen, if visible. Make notes of what is on the screen if it cannot be successfully photographed.
  - [ ] Do not remove any SIMM cards or micro SD storage cards.
- [ ] Be aware that certain cellular telephones can be remotely wiped clean; consider the use of a radiofrequency (RF) isolation bag (a lead-lined storage bag which prevents the phone from receiving a signal).
- [ ] Attempt to locate any instruction manuals, printed telephone bills, or passwords which may be associated with that particular phone.
- [ ] Determine if there is a regional computer forensics lab in your area. These labs will provide forensic examination of cellular telephones. Many of these labs provide a specialized kiosk which allows users to extract data from a cell phone, put it into a report, and burn the report to a CD or DVD.

Cellular Telephones in an Active Investigation

Investigative Considerations

Cellular telephones can be invaluable in an active, ongoing investigation. Most cellular telephone service companies provide a phone-tracking feature, which allows the subscriber of the telephone service to instantly locate any particular cellular phone on their account (if this feature is activated on the target phone). Consider utilizing this feature in abduction or kidnapping scenarios.

Most larger cellular telephone providers can provide law enforcement agencies with the "pinging" of cellular phones on their network in emergency situations. The pinging of the cell phone will provide an approximate location of where the cell phone is presently, and repeated pinging of the phone may establish a route the phone is traveling and a possible destination. Once an approximate location of the phone is identified, specialized equipment is available to more precisely determine where the phone is located.

- ☐ Determine, if possible, that the targeted cellular phone has the capability to be tracked.
  - ☐ Enlist the permission of the account subscriber to utilize the tracking feature.
  - ☐ Secure the necessary warrant or court order to track the cellular phone if consent is not granted by the subscriber to do so.
- ☐ Determine if any online accounts exist for the target cellular phone. These accounts may contain detailed call history, personal contact list, and historical data as to where the target phone has traveled and when calls were placed. Online accounts will also show the recipient telephone numbers of text messages sent by the target phone.
- ☐ Secure the necessary warrant or court order instructing the telephone service provider to provide the historical call information of the target phone. Most telephone service providers will provide an online template as to what information they require for their compliance with a legal order to turn over information.

Cellular Telephones in Nonactive Investigations

Investigative Considerations

The following information can be supplied by telephone service providers relative to the historical locations of the target phone.

- [ ] Subscriber information: Please note that with the availability of the "pay as you go" type of cellular telephone, the phone user often does not have to provide any identification to activate the cellular phone. Also, the actual user of the target cell phone may not be the subscriber, or the phone may have been stolen.
    - [ ] The telephone numbers dialed from the target phone
    - [ ] The date, time, and cell phone tower at which the outgoing calls were placed
    - [ ] The telephone numbers received by the target phone
    - [ ] The date, time, and cell phone tower at which the target phone received a call
    - [ ] The duration of the call
- [ ] Each cell phone tower has a unique identifying number associated with it. By consulting the resource guide provided by the particular telephone service provider, the latitude and longitude of the particular cell tower can be plotted on a map. Additionally, the direction of the cell phone from the cell tower can be determined with a reasonable amount of accuracy.
- [ ] Most telephone service providers can provide the above information in a conventional paper format or in an electronic format such as a spreadsheet file or CD. Electronic formats lend themselves to faster data analysis.
    - [ ] Ensure that you request their cell phone tower location guide, so the plotting of their towers can be conducted.
    - [ ] Telephone service providers may store this historical information for only a short period of time. Some will hold and protect the required information if they are contacted and advised that the necessary warrant or court orders are being prepared.
- [ ] The Microsoft Streets and Maps program allows the user to batch input latitude and longitude coordinates to plot cell phone towers on a printable map.

Notes

Hanging - Decorticate posturing
Decerebrate

845·429·0205 - Home
vernongebert@practicalhomicide.com

DNA Labs International
www.dnalabsinternational.com
Alison Nunes   954-426-5163

George Adams
Center for Human Identification
800·763·3147